C000303090

ESSENTIAL
COSTA BRAVA

Original text by Tony Kelly
Revised and updated by Mona Kraus

© AA Media Limited 2011
First published 2008. Content verified and updated 2011
ISBN 978-0-7495-6792-7

Published by AA Publishing, a trading name of AA Media Limited, whose registered office is Fanum House, Basing View, Basingstoke, Hampshire RG21 4EA. Registered number 06112600.

Colour separation: AA Digital Department
Printed and bound in Italy by Printer Trento S.r.l.

Find out more about AA Publishing and the wide range of services the AA provides by visiting our website at theAA.com/shop

A04193
Maps in this title supplied by Global Mapping, Brackley, UK. Copyright © Global Mapping/Cartografia

About this book

This book is divided into five sections.

The essence of the Costa Brava
pages 6–19
Introduction; Features; Food and drink; Short break

Planning pages 20–33
Before you go; Getting there; Getting around; Being there

Best places to see pages 34–55
The unmissable highlights of any visit to the Costa Brava

Best things to do pages 56–77
Good places to have lunch; places to take the children; best beaches; best golf courses and more

Exploring pages 78–185
The best places to visit in the Costa Brava, organized by area

Maps
All map references are to the maps on the covers. For example, Castellfollit de la Roca has the reference 🕂 4D – indicating the grid square in which it is to be found

Admission prices
Inexpensive (under €3.50)
Moderate (€3.50–€10)
Expensive (over €10)

Hotel prices
Prices are for a double room per night in summer including breakfast and 7 per cent VAT: € budget (under €75); €€ moderate (€75–€150); €€€ (over €150)

Restaurant prices
Prices are for a three-course meal per person without drinks and service:
€ budget (under €20); €€ moderate (€20–€40); €€€ (over €40)

Contents

The essence of...

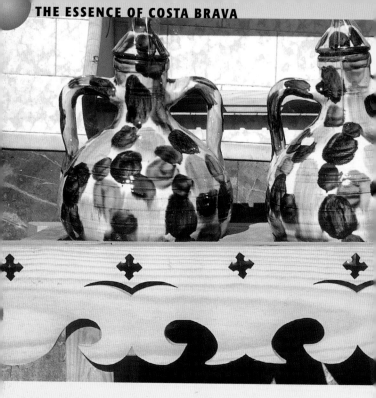

You cannot separate the Costa Brava from Catalonia. History has given the Catalans a fiercely independent spirit, looking outwards, to Europe, as much as in, to the Iberian peninsula. The first Greek and Roman settlers landed here; French art and architecture crossed into Spain over the Pyrenees. It is no surprise that this is where Spain's large-scale tourist industry began. The Catalans are courteous, businesslike, conservative and welcoming, but with little of the flamboyance of their Spanish neighbours. In the Mediterranean way, they know how to take life slowly – but also how to get things done.

features

Costa Brava – "the Wild Coast". The name was coined by a local journalist, Ferran Agulló, in 1908, gazing out at the rugged coastline of pine-clad cliffs and coves. At times you could be forgiven for thinking he was referring to the nightlife, rather than the scenery.

GEOGRAPHY AND CLIMATE

● The Costa Brava begins at Blanes, 60km (37 miles) north of Barcelona, and continues around the coast for 220km (137 miles) to the French border at Portbou.

● There are 119 official beaches, with a total length of 56km (35 miles) – a quarter of the entire coastline.

● The average summer temperature is 26°C (79°F), and there are more than 200 days of sunshine a year. The sea temperature reaches 24°C (75°F) in August and is pleasantly warm from June to October. The *tramuntana*, a cold north wind, can strike at any time.

GOVERNMENT AND ECONOMY

● The Costa Brava belongs to Girona province, itself part of Catalunya (Catalonia), a semi-autonomous region of Spain since 1979. Catalonia is the wealthiest region in Spain, producing around 20 per cent of the country's gross national product.

PEOPLE

● The population of the Costa Brava region rises from around 425,000 in winter to a million in summer. The capital, Girona, has a population of approximately 90,000. Catalonia has the highest population density of any region in Spain.

TOURISM

● More than five million foreign tourists visit the Costa Brava each year. The majority are from France, Germany and the UK. There is also a growing number of foreigners owning second homes in the region.

● The Costa Brava is the favourite holiday destination among Catalans, who make two million visits to the area each year.

● The Costa Brava can offer visitors a choice from around 40,000 hotel beds, 145 campsites and over 135,000 apartments.

food & drink

Catalan cooking is one of the great cuisines of Europe, with the produce of the sea and the mountains enhanced by many foreign influences. The Romans introduced olives and planted vines; the Arabs brought saffron, almonds and dried fruit. The essential flavours are Mediterranean – olive oil, garlic, onions, tomatoes, peppers – and the latest trend towards "modern Catalan" cuisine combines traditional ingredients with French and Italian styles.

MAIN MEALS

The most characteristic style of cooking is known as *mar i muntanya* (mountain and sea). This produces unusual combinations, like chicken with lobster, rabbit with snails and pigs' trotters stuffed with prawns. Paella comes into this category too – a mound of steaming saffron rice, which might be topped with just about any combination of meat, seafood and snails.

Meat is always excellent, especially veal from Girona and lamb from Ripoll. Duck might be accompanied by either turnips or pears. One famous meat dish is *escudella i carn d'olla*, a hearty boiled meat casserole that is traditionally served at Christmas; the broth is eaten with pasta shells as a starter, with the meat to follow. The Catalans are particularly proud of their many pork sausages: popular varieties include *botifarra*, *bisbe*, *llonganissa* and *fuet*. Some are eaten raw, like a salami, but *botifarra* is usually grilled and served with white beans.

Fish and seafood are served all along the coast, often simply grilled with a *romesco* (tomato, almond and pepper) sauce. Hake, monkfish and sole are widely available; sea bass and mullet are more expensive. *Suquet de peix* is a delicious casserole of white fish and potatoes, poached in white wine.

SNACKS, SALADS AND STARTERS

Tapas bars serve a bewildering range of snacks, from meatballs to octopus, in saucer-size portions. The classic bar snack is a plate of *pa amb tomàquet* – bread rubbed with tomato, drizzled with olive oil and topped with thin slices of cheese or cured mountain ham. Most bars keep a selection of *truitas* – cold potato omelettes, sometimes flavoured with spinach, artichoke or courgette. A Catalan salad *(amanida)* makes a meal in itself – piles of lettuce, tomato, olives and onions with a selection of cold meats, cheeses, tuna and egg. Other popular starters include *escalivada* (grilled

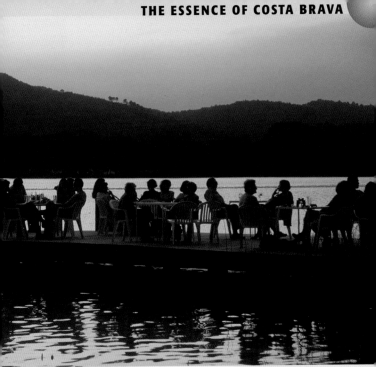

pepper and aubergine salad) and *esqueixada*, a salad topped with shredded salt cod.

DESSERTS

Spain is not known for its desserts but Catalonia produces two of the best – *crema catalana*, an egg custard with a caramelized sugar crust, and *mel i mató*, curd cheese with honey. In most eating places you are likely to be offered a choice between fresh fruit, ice cream and *flan* (caramel custard).

short break

If you only have a short time to visit the Costa Brava and would like to take home some unforgettable memories, you can do something local and capture the real flavour of the area. The following suggestions will give you a wide range of sights and experiences that won't take long, won't cost very much and will make your visit very special.

- **Follow the winding coast road** from Tossa de Mar to Sant Feliu (➤ 164–165), then explore the rocky coves around Begur and Palafrugell that gave the Costa Brava its name.

- **Go diving or snorkelling** in the waters around the Medes islands (➤ 100), where the reefs and caves harbour an abundance of underwater life.

● **Visit the fish markets** in Blanes, Palamós and Roses, then dine out on some of the freshest seafood (➤ 158–159, 166, 50–51).

● **Relax in the botanical gardens** at Cap Roig and Blanes (➤ 97, 159), where Mediterranean plants grow on cliffsides overlooking the sea.

● **Wander the back streets of Girona**, with its carefully restored Jewish quarter and medieval mansions (➤ 82–92).

● **Visit the surreal Dalí museum** in Figueres (➤ 52–53), then follow the Salvador Dalí trail from Portlligat to Puból (➤ 144–145).

● **Head for one of the inland towns on market day** for a real taste of Catalan life. One of the best is the Saturday market at Vic (➤ 172).

● **Browse in the pottery shops** of La Bisbal (➤ 95) and take home a souvenir of your visit.

● **Take a boat trip** along the coast around the wild northern coastline between Roses and Cap de Creus.

● **Join in a *sardana,*** Catalonia's traditional dance, which takes place at weekends or on festival days all over the region.

Planning

Before you go

WHEN TO GO

JAN	FEB	MAR	APR	MAY	JUN	JUL	AUG	SEP	OCT	NOV	DEC
13°C	14°C	16°C	19°C	21°C	25°C	27°C	27°C	25°C	22°C	16°C	14°C
55F	57°F	61°F	66°F	70°F	77°F	81°F	81°F	77°F	72°F	61°F	57°F

High season Low season

The above temperatures are the average daily maximum for each month on the coast. Sunshine is almost guaranteed throughout the summer, particularly during the peak tourist season of July and August. If you want to avoid the crowds but still enjoy warm, sunny weather, the best months to visit are May, June and September. These are also the best times for activities such as walking, cycling and golf. Between October and April, many hotels close their doors and resorts that are lively in summer have a distinct off-season feel.

Girona is busy throughout the year. Away from the coast, the weather is more unpredictable. You should always take warm clothes and be prepared for wind, rain and snow in mountain areas.

WHAT YOU NEED

					UK	Germany	USA	Netherlands
●	Required	Contact your travel agent or embassy for the current regulations regarding passports and visas. Your passport should be valid for at least six months beyond date of entry.						
○	Suggested							
▲	Not required							
Passport/National Identity Card					●	●	●	●
Visa (Regulations can change – check before you travel)					▲	▲	▲	▲
Onward or Return Ticket					▲	▲	●	▲
Health Inoculations					▲	▲	▲	▲
Health Documentation (➤ 23, Health Insurance)					●	●	●	●
Travel Insurance					○	○	●	○
Driving Licence (National)					●	●	●	●
Car Insurance Certificate					●	●	●	●

WEBSITES
www.costabrava.org

www.catalunyatourism.com

TOURIST OFFICES AT HOME

In the UK
Spanish Tourist Office
PO Box 4009, London W1A 6NB
☎ 020 7486 8077
www.spain.info

In the USA
Tourist Office of Spain
666 Fifth Avenue (35th Floor)

New York, NY 10103
☎ 212/265-8822

Tourist Office of Spain
8383 Wilshire Boulevard
Suite 960, Beverly Hills
CA 90211
☎ 323/658-7192
www.spain.info

HEALTH INSURANCE
Citizens of European Union countries are entitled to free reciprocal health care in Spain on production of an EHIC (European Health Insurance Card). Private medical insurance is still advisable for emergencies, and is essential for all non-European Union visitors.

ADVANCE PASSENGER INFORMATION (API)
Passengers on all flights to and from Spain now have to supply advance passenger information to the Spanish authorities – full given names, surname, nationality, date of birth and travel document details, namely a passport number. Some airports may have a self-service kiosk for this, otherwise staff at check-in desks will be able to collect the information.

TIME DIFFERENCES

GMT	Costa Brava	Germany	USA (NY)	Netherlands	Spain
12 noon	1PM	1PM	7AM	1PM	1PM

Like the rest of Spain, Catalonia is one hour ahead of Greenwich Mean Time (GMT+1), except from late March to late October, when summertime (GMT+2) operates.

NATIONAL HOLIDAYS

1 Jan *New Year's Day*
6 Jan *Epiphany*
Mar/Apr *Good Friday, Easter Monday*
1 May *Labour Day*
24 Jun *St John's Day*
15 Aug *Assumption of the Virgin*

11 Sep *Catalan National Day*
12 Oct *Spanish National Day*
1 Nov *All Saints' Day*
6 Dec *Constitution Day*
8 Dec *Feast of the Immaculate Conception*

25 Dec *Christmas Day*
26 Dec *St Stephen's Day*
Most shops, banks and offices close on these days, but many places stay open in the main resorts. Museums observe Sunday opening times.

WHAT'S ON WHEN

January *Els Tres Reis* (5–6 Jan): children across Catalonia receive their Christmas presents when the Three Kings arrive in towns and villages by boat or on horseback.

February *Carnestoltes*: pre-Lenten carnival parades (see opposite).

March/April *Setmana Santa* (Holy Week): on the evening of Maundy Thursday, men and boys dressed as skeletons march through Verges, near Torroella de Montgrí, performing a medieval "dance of death". Girona's Good Friday procession re-enacts Christ's death, with his crucified body carried to the cathedral by actors dressed as Roman soldiers. There is also a crucifixion ceremony on Good Friday in Sant Hilari Sacalm.

Festa de Sant Jordi (23 Apr): book and flower markets are set up in the streets in honour of Catalonia's patron, St George. The biggest festivities take place along the Rambla in Girona.

May *Carroussel Costa Brava* (Whit Sunday): Palafrugell's Spring Festival was begun in 1963 to continue the carnival traditions following its prohibition. The highlight is the parade of floats on the Sunday afternoon.

June *Festa de Sant Joan* (23–24 Jun): the eve of the feast of St John is marked with bonfires and firework parties all over Catalonia.

July *Cantada d'Havaneres* (1st Sat): traditional sea-shanties on the beach at Calella de Palafrugell.

Aplec de la Sardana (2nd Sun): the biggest *sardana* festival takes place in Olot.

Mare de Déu del Carme (16 Jul): processions of fishing boats in the main ports in honour of the protector of fishermen.

Festa de Santa Cristina (24–26 Jul): Moorish dancing and a mass pilgrimage by boat from Lloret de Mar to the hermitage of Santa Cristina.

August *Cantada d'Havaneres* (1st Sat): traditional sea shanties on the beach at Llafranc.

Mayor's Sardana (16 Aug): open spiral dance held at night in Amer, west of Girona.

September *Festa del Tura* (8 Sep): processions of giants, dwarves and hobby-horses in the streets of Olot.

La Diada (11 Sep): Catalonia's national day is marked all over the region by fireworks, street parades and *sardana* dancing.

October *Festa de Sant Narcís* (late Oct): a fortnight of festivities in Girona, featuring bullfights, bonfires and parades of giants.

December *Nadal* (Christmas, 24–25 Dec): midnight Mass is celebrated in churches across the region.

Carnival The pre-Lenten carnival, with its riotous street parades and fancy-dress balls, was banned under the Franco dictatorship, but has returned with a vengeance. Every town on the Costa Brava seems to organize its own Carnival festivities. The processions of floats at Platja d'Aro and Palamós, on the weekend before Shrove Tuesday, are some of the biggest in Spain. Carnival ends with the "burial of the sardine", signifying the end of winter.

Getting there

BY AIR

Barcelona (El Prat) Airport

100km (62 miles) to Girona

🚃	2 hours
🚌	N/A
🚗	90 minutes

Girona-Costa Brava Airport

11km (7 miles) to Girona

🚃	N/A
🚌	30 minutes
🚗	20 minutes

Girona-Costa Brava airport (☎ 972 18 66 00) is served by regular flights from London, Paris, Rome and other European cities. There are several flights a day from the UK by Ryanair (☎ 0871 246 0000; www.ryanair.com) as well as additional charter flights in summer. Barcelona Bus (☎ 902 36 15 50) operates shuttle buses from the airport into central Girona and also to the main resorts. A wider range of scheduled carriers, including the Spanish national airline Iberia, fly into Barcelona airport.

BY CAR
European route E15 connects Paris to Barcelona and travels through the Costa Brava region. From Paris, it follows the A6 motorway to Lyon, then the A7 to Orange and A9 to Perpignan, before crossing the border at La Jonquera, where it becomes the Spanish AP7. It is best to allow two days for the journey. Alternatively, take a car ferry from the UK to Northern Spain and join the Spanish motorway network from Bilbao to Barcelona.

BY TRAIN
Girona and Figueres are both stops on the high-speed rail link from Paris to Barcelona, which crosses into Spain at Portbou. The Elipsos train network links Paris, Zurich and Milan with Girona and Barcelona, using comfortable overnight "train hotels". For UK bookings, contact Rail Europe (0870 837 1371; www.raileurope.co.uk).

Getting around

PUBLIC TRANSPORT

Trains The main line from Barcelona to France passes through the Costa Brava region, with regular stops at Girona, Figueres and Portbou. There is also a branch line linking Barcelona and Girona with Blanes. For information on train services, call RENFE (tel: 902 24 02 02; www.renfe.es).

Buses A wide network of local bus routes, operated by a number of private companies, such as Sarfa (www.sarfa.com), Ampsa (www.ampsa.org) and Teisa (www.teisa-bus.com), connects Girona and Figueres with the main towns and villages of the Costa Brava. Extra routes connect the coastal resorts in summer. Timetables change, so check with your local tourist office or at the nearest bus station.

Boats A regular boat service connects the resorts of Blanes, Lloret de Mar and Tossa de Mar between April and October, with some boats continuing north as far as Palamós. There are departures at least hourly, calling at various beaches along the way, so you can use this service for day-trips to nearby beaches and coves. There are also a number of cruises in summer from all the major resorts, including Cadaqués, Roses, Empúriabrava, L'Estartit and Sant Feliu de Guíxols – details can be found on the quayside at noticeboards and ticket kiosks. One popular trip is the cruise to the Illes Medes (Medes Islands) on a glass-hulled boat from L'Estartit (➤ 99).

FARES AND TICKETS

Students/Youths Holders of an International Student Identity Card (ISIC) may be able to obtain some concessions on travel and entrance fees. Anyone under 26 or belonging to a national youth hostel organization can stay cheaply at the hostels *(albergues de joventut)* in Girona, Banyoles, Olot and Empúries.

Senior citizens There are few specific discounts available for senior citizens, though it is always worth checking at museums and tourist attractions. A number of hotels and tour operators offer economical deals on long-stay winter holidays, when the savings in the cost of fuel bills can almost wipe out the cost of the trip.

TAXIS

Taxis can be hired at ranks or by flagging down a taxi with a green light on the roof. Prices are good, but there are supplements for late-night, weekend and public holiday travel, as well as for luggage and long-distance journeys.

DRIVING

- The Spanish drive on the right side of the road.

- Seat belts must be worn at all times. Children under 12 must use an approved child seat/harness.

- Random breath-testing is carried out. Never drive under the influence of alcohol.

- Fuel *(gasolina)* is sold in various grades, including unleaded *(sense plomb)* and super-unleaded and diesel *(gasoil)*. A few petrol stations are self-service but most have an attendant. Credit cards are widely accepted and at some you can pay at the pump using your card.

- Speed limits are as follows:
  Motorways (autopistas – toll payable): 120kph (74mph)
  Main roads: 100kph (62mph)
  Minor roads 90kph/56mph)
  Urban roads: 50kph (31mph)

- If you are driving your own car in Spain it is a good idea to take out European breakdown cover. Members of AIT-affiliated motoring clubs, including the AA, can use the services of the Real Automóvil Club de España (RACE, tel: 902 40 45 45) or Real Automóvil Club de Catalunya (RACC, tel: 902 10 61 06). Car-rental firms provide their own rescue service.

CAR RENTAL

The leading international car rental companies have offices at Barcelona and Girona airports. There are local companies in the resorts. Keep hire documents, your driving licence and your passport with you at all times.

Being there

TOURIST OFFICES

Blanes
Passeig de Catalunya 2
☎ 972 33 03 48

Figueres
Plaça del Sol s/n
☎ 972 50 31 55

Girona
Carrer Joan Maragall 2
☎ 872 97 59 75

Lloret de Mar
Passeig Camprodón i Arrieta 1
☎ 972 36 47 35

Olot
Carrer del'Hospici 8
☎ 972 26 01 41

Palafrugell
Carrer Carrilet 2
☎ 972 30 02 28

Tossa de Mar
Avinguda del Pelegrí 25
☎ 972 34 01 08

Vic
Carrer Ciutat 4
☎ 938 86 20 91

The above offices are open throughout the year. Most towns and villages have offices open in summer; look out for the international "L" sign.

The staff are usually multilingual and helpful and can supply you with local maps and guides.

Information about the Costa Brava can also be found at www.costabrava.org

MONEY

The euro (€) is the official currency of Spain, divided into 100 cents (or *centesimi*). Coins come in denominations of 1, 2, 5, 10, 20 and 50 cents, 1 and 2 euros, and bank notes come in denominations of 5, 10, 20, 50, 100, 200 and 500 euros (the last two are rarely seen). The notes and one side of the coins are the same throughout the European single currency zone, but each country has a different design on one face of each of the coins. Bank notes and coins from any of the other countries can be used in Spain.

TIPS/GRATUITIES

Yes ✓ No ✕

Restaurants	✓	10%
Cafés/bars	✓	change
Taxis	✓	10%
Tour guides (discretionary)	✓	€1–2
Chambermaids/porters	✓	€1–2
Toilet attendants	✕	

POSTAL SERVICES

Post offices *(Correus)* are generally open Monday–Saturday 9am–1pm.
Stamps *(segells)* can also be bought at kiosks and at tobacconists'
shops *(estancs)*.

TELEPHONES

Public telephones take euro coins as well as phonecards *(teletarjetas)*,
which can be bought at post offices or tobacconists. Most also accept
credit cards. The cheap rate for international calls is weekdays 10pm–8am,
after 2pm Saturday and all day Sunday.

International dialling codes

From Spain to
UK: 00 44
Germany: 00 49

USA & Canada: 00 1
Netherlands: 00 31

Emergency telephone numbers

Police (Policía Nacional/Mosso
d'Esquadra): 091
Fire (Bombers): 085

Ambulance (Ambulància): 061
In any emergency you can ring 112

EMBASSIES AND CONSULATES

UK: ☎ 93 366 6200
Germany: ☎ 93 292 10 00

USA: ☎ 93 280 2227
Netherlands: ☎ 93 363 54 20

HEALTH ADVICE

Sun advice Avoid the midday sun and use a high-factor sun block.
Children are particularly vulnerable and should always wear a hat.

Drugs Prescription and non-prescription drugs are available from pharmacies *(farmàcias)*, distinguished by a large green cross. Recreational drugs, which you may be offered at nightclubs in the larger resorts, are illegal and should be avoided.

Safe water Tap water is generally safe to drink, but mineral water is cheap and easy to buy, either sparkling *(amb gas)* or still *(sense gas)*.

PERSONAL SAFETY

In an emergency, ask for the nearest police station *(comissaria)* and speak to the Policía Nacional, known in Catalonia as the Mossos d'Esquadra. Take sensible precautions to avoid crime:

● Don't carry more cash than you need.
● Never leave valuables on the beach or by the pool.
● Always lock your car with any valuables out of sight in the boot.
● Beware of pickpockets in crowded markets or tourist sights.
Police assistance: ☎ 112 from any call box

ELECTRICITY

The power supply in Spain is 220–225 volts. Sockets accept two-round-pin style plugs. Visitors from the UK require an adaptor and US visitors a transformer for appliances operating on 100–120 volts.

OPENING HOURS

● Shops   ● Main post offices   ● Pharmacies
● Banks   ● Museums/monuments

9 AM	10 AM	11 AM	12 PM	1 PM	2 PM	3 PM	4 PM	5 PM	6 PM
9.30	10.30	11.30	12.30	1.30	2.30	3.30	4.30	5.30	

Most shops close Sat evening and all day Sun, though shops in larger resorts may be open daily throughout the day. Banks open Sat mornings in winter only. There is always one pharmacist on duty in the main towns; details are in local papers and shop windows. Most markets open in the morning and start closing mid-afternoon. Many museums close on Mon.

LANGUAGE

Although Spanish is still universally understood, it is Catalan that you are most likely to see and hear on the streets. It is spoken in Valencia, Andorra, the Balearic islands and parts of the French Pyrenees, as well as in Catalonia. Many Catalan words look like their equivalents in French or Spanish – but the sound of the language is utterly distinct.

hotel	*hotel*	bath/shower	*bany/dutxa*
campsite	*càmping*	washbasin/toilet	*lavabo/vàter*
apartment	*apartament*	balcony	*balcó*
single room	*habitació senzilla*	sea view	*vista al mar*
double room	*habitació doble*	one night	*una nit*
bank	*banc*	banknote	*bitllet de banc*
exchange bureau	*oficina de canvi*	credit card	*tarjeta de crèdit*
cashier	*caixer*	change	*canvi*
travellers' cheque	*xec de viatge*	how much?	*quant és?*
foreign currency	*moneda estrangera*	post office	*correus*
breakfast	*esmorzar*	white wine/red wine	*vi blanc/vi negre*
lunch/dinner	*dinar/sopar*	water	*aigua*
menu/set menu	*carta/menú*	sparkling/still	*amb gas/sense gas*
waiter/waitress	*cambrer/cambrera*	beer	*cervesa*
airport/aeroplane	*aeroport/avió*	return	*anar i tornar*
station/train	*estació/tren*	taxi/car	*taxi/cotxe*
bus	*autobús*	garage	*garatge*
boat	*vaixell*	petrol station	*gasolinera*
ticket	*bitllet*	motorway	*autopista*
yes/no	*si/no*	welcome	*benvinguts*
please/thank you	*sisplau/gràcies*	open/closed	*obert/tancat*
hello/goodbye	*hola/adéu*	I don't understand	*no ho entenc*
good morning	*bon dia*	do you speak English?	*parla anglès?*
good afternoon	*bona tarda*		
goodnight	*bona nit*	I don't speak Catalan	*no parlo català*
excuse me/sorry	*perdoni/ho sento*		

Best places to see

1 Besalú

A well-preserved medieval town centre at the heart of the region, with several Romanesque churches and the only Jewish bath house in Spain.

This small town at the confluence of the Fluvià and Capellada rivers was the historic capital of the Garrotxa region, ruled for more than 200 years by a dynasty established by Wilfred the Hairy. After the 12th century its importance declined, but following its declaration as a National Historic Monument in 1966 it has been restored to its former glory.

Come here on a Tuesday morning, when the porticoed central square, Plaça Llibertat, is buzzing with chatter and the market stalls are piled high with flowers, fruit and cheese, and you realize that this is still very much a working town. Along the cobbled streets that fan out from the square are delicatessens and antiques shops, set among medieval arches, columns and Gothic windows. Of several Romanesque churches, the most impressive is the monastery church of Sant Pere, with a pair of stone lions adorning its facade.

The symbol of Besalú is its angled bridge over the Fluvià, built in the 11th century and destroyed several

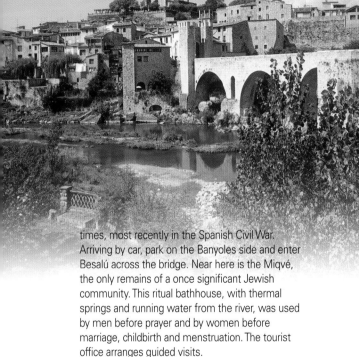

times, most recently in the Spanish Civil War.
Arriving by car, park on the Banyoles side and enter
Besalú across the bridge. Near here is the Miqvé,
the only remains of a once significant Jewish
community. This ritual bathhouse, with thermal
springs and running water from the river, was used
by men before prayer and by women before
marriage, childbirth and menstruation. The tourist
office arranges guided visits.

🚪 5D 🍴 Curia Reial (€€, ➤ 59) 🚌 From Figueres, Girona
and Olot ❓ Market on Tue; Festa dels Dolors, evening
procession on the Fri before Palm Sunday; *sardana* dancing
on Easter Sunday; Festa Major, last weekend in Sep. A
1-hour miniature train tour in summer includes a guided
walk and visit to the Miqvé (moderate)
ℹ️ Plaça Llibertat 1, tel: 972 59 12 40

2 Cadaqués

This fishing village and stylish resort has long attracted a curious mixture of artists, tourists and people seeking an alternative way of life.

Cadaqués appears at first sight to be a typical Mediterranean fishing village. It still is a fishing village, but it is much more than that. Picasso spent some time here in the early 20th century, but it was Salvador Dalí who really put Cadaqués on the map. His father came from here; it was here that he met his wife; and it was near here, at Portlligat, that he eventually settled down, attracted by the light, the remoteness and the rugged beauty of Spain's most easterly village.

There are reminders of Dalí everywhere: a statue on the seafront, a sundial on the facade of a hotel, the logo of the L'Hostal bar. In the 1960s, when hippies and intellectuals flocked to Dalí's side, Cadaqués was known as Spain's St-Tropez. It holds the same appeal for many people today.

There are several art galleries and stylish boutiques. The **Museu de Cadaqués** features contemporary Catalan artists. The old town of steep and narrow streets winds its way from the waterfront up to the church of Santa Maria, with its baroque reredos.

🕂 11C 🍴 Cuatro (€€, ➤ 58) 🚌 From Figueres and Roses
❓ Market on Mon; Mare de Déu del Carme, procession of
fishing boats on 16 Jul; international music and arts festival,
Jul and Aug
ℹ️ Carrer Cotxe 2A, tel: 972 25 83 15

Museu de Cadaqués

✉️ Carrer Narcís Monturiol 15 ☎ 972 25 88 77 🕐 Hours
vary according to exhibitions. Usually, summer 10:30–1:30,
4–8 ✋ Moderate

3 Castell Gala Dalí

The castle that Salvador Dalí bought as a refuge for his wife has become a shrine to her memory and to the couple's bizarre relationship.

When Salvador and Gala Dalí were in exile in Italy during the Spanish Civil War, the painter promised his wife that he would one day buy her a castle. Thirty years later, he acquired this Gothic and Renaissance castle in the village of Púbol. Dalí wanted Gala to be able to get away from him, with her lovers if necessary, and insisted that he would never enter the castle without her permission.

The castle was in a state of disrepair and Dalí set about recreating it. The result is a typically Dalíesque mixture of the grotesque, the beautiful and the absurd. Classical statues in the garden share space with elephant figures sculpted from cement; 17th-century tapestries hang beside *trompe l'oeil* painted radiators and huge Dalí canvases. Everywhere you look there are portraits of Gala, and her initial G is frequently worked into the design.

Gala spent little time in her castle, arriving for short stays each summer but continuing to live with Dalí in Portlligat (➤ 142–143). When she died in 1982, her body was driven to Púbol and buried in the crypt – with a stuffed giraffe looking on. Dalí moved into her room, but two years later he set fire to the bed and, despite a life-saving operation, he

was never to return to the castle. The Cadillac in which he insisted on leaving Púbol – he refused to take an ambulance – still sits in the garage. Dalí left the castle to the Spanish state and it was opened to the public as a museum in 1996.

➕ 20G ☎ 972 48 86 55 🕐 15 Jun–15 Sep daily 10–8; 15 Mar–14 Jun, 16 Sep–1 Nov Tue–Sun 10–6; 2 Nov–31 Dec Tue–Sun 10–5 ✋ Moderate 🍴 Can Bosch (€, ➤ 123) in Púbol 🚌 Buses between Girona and Palafrugell pass 2km (1.2 miles) away

4 Empúries

An ancient Greek and Roman settlement on the shores of the Gulf of Roses, where Spain first came into contact with wider European culture.

It was the Greeks who first established a trading post *(emporion)* here on what was then an island; contact between Greek settlers and indigenous tribes led to the development of the Iberian culture. The Romans anchored at Empúries in 218BC, the first step on the route to the colonization of Spain. The Roman city of Emporiae was abandoned in the 3rd century AD and only rediscovered by archaeologists in 1908. Much of it has still to be excavated.

The remains of the Roman city show how much Spanish town planning owes to Roman influence. The forum at the centre, the forerunner of the Plaça Major, would once have been surrounded by

arcades; there were temples at one end and a main street leading to the city walls. Even the amphitheatre outside the walls has its equivalent in today's bullring or football stadium.

Below is the Greek city, dominated by a statue of

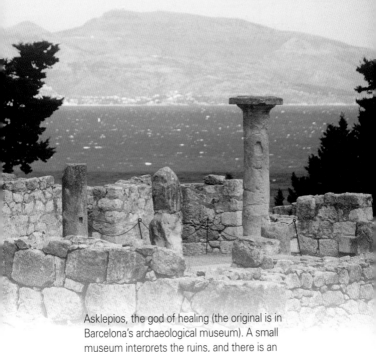

Asklepios, the god of healing (the original is in Barcelona's archaeological museum). A small museum interprets the ruins, and there is an excellent audio-visual show. Afterwards you can walk along the seafront, past the original Greek jetty, to the village of Sant Martí d'Empúries, site of the first Greek settlement.

✚ 10E ✉ 1km (0.5 miles) north of L'Escala ☎ 972 77 02 08 🕐 Jun–Sep daily 10–8; Oct–May daily 10–6 ✋ Inexpensive; extra charge for audio-visual show 🍴 Snack bar (€) on site, restaurants (€–€€) in Sant Martí d'Empúries 🚌 To L'Escala from Figueres, Girona and Palafrugell

5 Girona Old Town

The restoration of the old quarter at the heart of Girona has been one of the great success stories of modern Catalonia.

Following its modernization over recent years, Girona is now considered to be one of the most desirable places to live in Catalonia. The political and cultural renaissance since 1980 has been accompanied by an architectural revival and a determination to show this historic city at its best. Dilapidated convents have been given new life as museums and art galleries, the university has been restored to its 16th-century home, and the narrow streets of the medieval Jewish district, the Call Jueu (► 84), have been carefully restored.

This is a city for strolling, wandering at random among the maze of streets and going wherever a hidden archway or flight of steps leads you. Sun and shade, iron and stone, courtyards and balconies, narrow alleys and wide open squares, all come together here in perfect harmony.

Girona is at its most enchanting in the streets of the old guilds. Between Plaça de l'Oli and Plaça del Vi, once the oil and wine markets, lies a network of narrow lanes, each named after a medieval trade. Carrer de l'Argenteria was once lined with silversmiths, Carrer de Mercaders with merchants, Carrer de les Ferreries Velles with blacksmiths and Carrer Peixateries Velles with fishmongers. Their places may have been taken by trendy cafes and boutiques, but the streets are still appealing.

✚ *Girona 6d*

🍴 Café L'Arcada (€), Rambla de la Llibertat 38

🚌 Girona bus station, 1km (0.5 miles) away

🚉 Girona, 1km (0.5 miles) away

❓ Holy Week procession on Good Friday

ℹ Carrer Joan Maragall 2, tel: 872 97 59 75

6 Monestir de Sant Pere de Rodes

Some claim that the monastery was built on the site of a Roman temple, but the more colourful story concerns Pope Boniface IV (608–615) and St Peter's head. With Rome under threat, the Pope ordered the church's most sacred relics to be sent to Spain for safe-keeping. When the time came to retrieve them, the head was nowhere to be found, so a monastery was built on the site here and dedicated to the saint. There are records of a monastery here from AD878 – though recent excavations suggest that the site was in use long before that. The present church, dating from 1022, marks the transition to Romanesque architecture in Catalonia. The original cloister, its galleries decorated with murals, is covered by an upper cloister on the same level as the church. This was an important place of pilgrimage throughout the Middle Ages, but fell into decline after the 14th century. The last monks left in 1798.

There are good views of the monastery from the chapel of Santa Elena, all that remains of the village that grew up around the church. For the best views, climb the path behind the

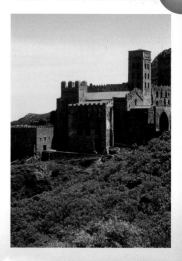

monastery to the ruined castle of Sant Salvador. Look down over the monastery and out to sea, then turn to see the Pyrenees on the horizon. The sunrises up here are magical.

✚ 10C ✉ Camí del Monestir s/n ☎ 972 38 75 59 🕐 Jun–Sep Tue–Sun 10–8; Oct–May Tue–Sun 10–5:30 ✋ Moderate (free on Tue) 🍴 Cafe-restaurant (€) 🚌 El Port de la Selva (5km/3 miles) 🚉 Vilajuïga (8km/5 miles)

7 Parc Natural de l'Aiguamolls de l'Empordà

This wetland nature reserve provides a refuge for wildlife and migrant birds and a peaceful haven for visitors escaping from the crowded beaches.

Once upon a time, marshes covered the coastal plain; Empúries (➤ 42–43) was an island and the Montgrí mountains were surrounded by fens. As the population grew, the marshes disappeared, at first as a result of agriculture and lately because of the increase in tourism. The building of the marina on former marshland at Empúriabrava (➤ 139) galvanized environmentalists into action, leading to the creation of this natural park in 1983.

Carp, mullet and eel thrive in the lakes; there are badgers, newts and voles, and otters are being reintroduced. Above all, the Empordà marshes are an important refuge for aquatic and migrant birds. Herons, ducks and geese live on the ponds; other species that breed here include the stone-curlew and the black-winged stilt. This is Spain's only nesting ground for the garganey, a rare species of duck. Seabirds flock here in winter, and during the main migrant seasons (March to May and August to October), it is possible to see 100 species in a day.

At the information centre in **El Cortalet** you can pick up leaflets and maps, and hire out binoculars, field guides and wheelchairs. There are two easy, waymarked trails that start from here, with hides overlooking the lagoons; except during the nesting season (April to mid-June), they can be combined with a walk along the beach in a two-hour circular trail.

➕ 9D
El Cortalet
✉ Off the road from Castelló d'Empúries to Sant Pere Pescador ☎ 972 45 42 22 🕐 Trails open at all times
🅿 Free (charge for car parking) 🚌 Castelló d'Empúries
❓ Keep to paths; be prepared for flooding in winter
ℹ Apr–Sep daily 9:30–2, 4:30–7; Oct–Mar 9:30–2, 3:30–6

8 Roses

A fishing port and ancient Greek colony, Roses has become the tourist capital of the northern Costa Brava.

With 4km (2.5 miles) of sandy beach at the head of a great sweeping bay, Roses is the perfect setting for a bucket-and-spade holiday. The sheltered waters are ideal for watersports, with windsurfing, sailing and waterskiing all available. There are also several smaller coves, beginning with Canyelles and Almadrava, 3km (2 miles) beyond the fishing harbour to the southeast. A hair-raising drive across a rugged landscape leads to the remote creek of Cala Montjoi; on the way you pass the Creu d'en Cobertella, the largest prehistoric burial chamber in Catalonia, dating from 3000BC.

Roses was founded in the 8th century BC by Greek settlers, who named it Rhodes after their homeland, but it was the Romans who developed the fishing industry that led to the town's wealth. It is still an important fishing port. With 50 hotels, 5 campsites and dozens of restaurants and bars, it is a little too lively for some; but if you want a

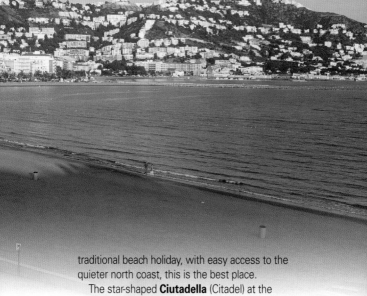

traditional beach holiday, with easy access to the quieter north coast, this is the best place.

The star-shaped **Ciutadella** (Citadel) at the entrance to town is a 16th-century fortress on the site of the original Greek city, with Roman and medieval remains within its walls – you can clamber over the ruins and look down into the moat. Another ruined castle, east of town, stands on the slopes of Puig Rom hill. Climb this hill at sunset for romantic views over the Bay of Roses with the snow-capped Pyrenees in the distance.

✚ 10C 🍴 La Llar (€€€, ➤ 155) 🚌 From Cadaqués and Figueres 🚢 Trips to Cadaqués, Cap de Creus and Cala Montjoi in summer ❓ Market on Sun; Mare del Déu del Carme, procession of fishing boats 16 Jul

🚩 Avinguda de Rhode 77, tel: 972 10 36 36

Ciutadella de Roses

☎ 972 15 14 66 🕐 Jun–Sep Tue–Sat 10–8; Oct–May Tue–Sat, 10–6, Sun 10–2 ✋ Inexpensive

9 Teatre-Museu Dalí

The memorial that Salvador Dalí created for himself in his home town of Figueres is a journey through the imagination of a tortured genius.

This is one of the most visited museums in Spain – but is it really a museum at all? Dalí, its creator, denied that it was, calling it "a gigantic surrealist object". Even the name theatre-museum has two meanings. It is built on the ruins of an old theatre, where Dalí had his first exhibition at the age of 14; but it is also a theatre because of the way we are meant to respond. Dalí did not want captions, or a catalogue; he wanted the "audience" to be free to create their own surrealist experience.

From outside the view is dominated by the transparent dome on the roof, together with Dalí's trademark eggs on the facade. Once inside, you are drawn to the courtyard, with its central sculpture, *Rainy Taxi*, featuring a giant model of Dalí's wife Gala standing on the bonnet of a black Cadillac. Some things you cannot miss – like the Mae West room, where a sofa and two fireplaces are turned by means of a lens into the pouting face of the legendary actress. Sooner or later you reach the crypt, where Dalí is buried; Dalí spent his last years in the Torre Galatea, and on his deathbed told the Mayor of Figueres he wanted to be buried in his theatre, rather than with Gala in her castle at Púbol. A separate exhibition dedicated to Dalí's jewellery is now open.

✚ 8C ✉ Plaça Gala-Salvador Dalí 5, Figueres ☎ 972 67 75 00 🕐 Jun daily 9:30–5:45; Jul–Sep daily 9–7:45; Oct, Mar–May Tue–Sun 9:30–5:45; Nov–Feb Tue–Sun 10:30–5:45 💶 Expensive 🚌 Figueres bus station, 1km (0.5 miles) away 🚉 Figueres, 1km (0.5 miles) away ❓ Night-time opening in Aug, 10–12:30

10 Tossa de Mar

The remains of a fortified medieval village look down on a horseshoe beach, making Tossa the most attractive of the Costa Brava resorts.

One resort on the crowded southern coast stands out head and shoulders above its neighbours. The beach alone would be enough to draw visitors, with safe swimming and sheltered sunbathing in an idyllic bay, and several smaller coves within easy reach. But what makes Tossa special is its walled medieval village (Vila Vella), standing proudly above the bay as it has done for more than 800 years.

Climb up from the main beach, Platja Gran, pausing to glance back at the sea through the arched window of an abandoned church, and you soon reach this attractive village. It was established in 1186 by the Abbot of Ripoll on the promontory of Mont Guardí. Beneath here, just behind the beach, is the Vila Nova (New Town), a warren of back streets and 19th-century houses around the parish church.

Tossa was one of the first places on the Costa Brava to attract foreign visitors. The painter Marc Chagall spent the summer of 1934 here and called it his "blue paradise". The **Museu Municipal,** in the former Abbot's palace, contains letters from Chagall, who was delighted that the museum was to display one of his paintings. Also worth a visit is the Mediterranean Lighthouse Interpretation Centre in the old lighthouse.

🕂 20L 🏨 Santa Marta (€€, ➤ 59) 🚌 From Lloret de Mar (and from Girona in summer) 🚢 South coast resorts in summer ❓ Market Thu

ℹ️ Avinguda del Pelegrí 25, tel: 972 34 01 08

Museu Municipal

✉️ Plaça Roig i Soler 1 ☎ 972 34 07 09 🕐 Oct–May Tue–Sat 10–2, 4–6, Sun 10–2; Jun–Sep daily 10–8

✋ Inexpensive

Best things to do

Good places to have lunch

Aiguablava (€€)

The Hotel Aiguablava's Grill Room is a top-class restaurant, known for its excellent cuisine and highly professional service.

✉ Platja de Fornells s/n, Begur ☎ 972 62 21 12 ⏲ Mar–Oct

Boira (€–€€)

Tapas downstairs as well as an upstairs restaurant with romantic views over the river.

✉ Plaça Independència 17, Girona ☎ 972 21 96 05 ⏲ Daily 1–4, 8:30–11 or later

Cap de Creus (€–€€)

The setting is fabulous, close to the lighthouse with magnificent views. Specialities are fresh fish and Indian cuisine.

✉ Cap de Creus ☎ 972 19 90 05 ⏲ Mon–Fri 12–7:30, Sat–Sun 12–11:30

Cuatro (€€)

Seafront restaurant serving good Catalan cuisine, with vegetarian options.

✉ Passeig Marítim 4, Cadaqués ☎ 972 15 91 07 ⏲ Daily 12:30–4, 7:30–11. Normally closed Jan–Feb

Curia Reial (€€)

Hearty meat dishes and "volcanic cuisine" feature on the menu, as well as a good set meal.

✉ Plaça Llibertat, Besalú ☎ 972 59 02 63 🕓 Lunch and dinner. Closed Tue

Durán (€€)

Top-notch Catalan cooking in Salvador Dalí's old haunt, which is decorated with tiles, old lamps and photographs of the artist.

✉ Carrer Lasauca 5, Figueres ☎ 972 50 12 50 🕓 Daily 12:45–4, 8:30–11

El Port (€–€€€)

Fresh fish and seafood from the neighbouring market beneath the harbour walls.

✉ Esplanada del Port, Blanes ☎ 972 33 48 19 🕓 Daily 5am–midnight

La Riera (€)

Hearty Catalan cooking using local produce. Try some of the specialities included in the gourmet menu.

✉ Plaça de les Voltes 3, Peratallada ☎ 972 634142 🕓 Lunch and dinner. Closed Tue in winter

Santa Marta (€€)

Housed in a medieval building in the old fortress, Santa Marta is known for its innovative cuisine.

✉ Carrer Francesc Aromir 2, Tossa de Mar ☎ 972 340472 🕓 Easter–Sep lunch and dinner Thu–Tue

Les Voltes (€€€)

Long-established, family-run restaurant offering an extensive menu of meat and fish dishes. Especially recommended for its outdoor seating under the arcades, overlooking the sea – idyllic on a warm summer's day.

✉ Les Voltes 7, Calella de Palafrugell ☎ 972 61 55 48 🕓 Daily 1–4, 8–11

Top activities

Aerial Sports: thrilling hot-air balloon flights over different parts of the region give a bird's-eye view of the area's magnificent scenery. You can also practise paragliding, delta- and hang-gliding.
Kon-Tiki Viatges en Globus ☎ 935 15 60 60;
www.globuskontiki.com

Cycling and mountain biking: from the hinterland to the coastal areas, the Empordà region offers magnificent scenery and challenging opportunities for cycling. The Baix Emporda Cycle Tourism Network covers an area with over 300km (185 miles) of cycle tracks.
For further information try
www.turismedecatalunya.com/cicloturisme

Diving, snorkelling and kayaking: the Medes Islands Marine Reserve, just off L'Estartit, is the place for diving and snorkelling enthusiasts. These and other activities, such as kayaking, are offered by Medaqua.
Medaqua ✉ Passeig Maritim 16, L'Estartit
☎ 972 75 20 43; www.medaqua.com

Horseback riding: another pleasurable way to explore the Costa Brava's impressive landscapes is on horseback. Numerous riding schools offer trips in the countryside and along the beach. Rides from Begur are organized by Hipica Begur. You can also contact local tourist offices for information on riding schools in the region.
Hipica Begur ☎ 650 32 38 48;
www.hipicabegur.com.

Sailing: seaside resorts with centres offering a range of nautical activities include the Medes Islands (L'Estartit) and Bay of Palamós-Calonge-Sant Antoni, where expert tuition is offered.
Associacio D'Estacions Nautiques de Cataluna; www.catalunya.info

Skiing: La Molina and Vall de Núria are popular winter-sports centres in the Pyrenees, near Ripoll.
Federacio Catala d'Esports d'Hivern; www.fceh.org

Swimming: swimming in the blue sparkling waters of the Mediterranean is the main draw to the Costa Brava in summer, with its variety of beaches, from long sandy stretches to strings of small bays and hidden rocky coves. Remember to observe warning flags.

Walking and hiking: with a wide range of signposted trails, there are countless possibilities for walking, both inland and by the sea. The Camí de Ronda (patrol walk) covers a very beautiful coastal route, with spectacular views over the Mediterranean.
Associacio Catalana d'Empreses de Senderismo ☎ 973 64 24 44; www.empresesdesenderisme.com

Waterskiing: many resorts along the coast provide equipment and expert tuition for waterskiing. Funtastic has a good sports centre in Platja de Riells, L'Escala.
Funtastic ☎ 972 774184; www.funtastic-emporda.com

Windsurfing: you can practise this in most resorts, in particular the Bay of Roses. Equipment and tuition are available from Club Mistral (www.club-mistral.com). Other centres are at Santa Susann, Pals, L'Estartit and Llfranch.
www.bluedome.co.uk/costabrava/windsurfing.html

a drive from Banyoles

This drive takes you into the heart of the Garrotxa, the region of dormant volcanoes just inland from Banyoles.

Start by the sports stadium on Carrer Alfonso XII, between central Banyoles and the lake, and take the main road heading north with the lake on your left.

After 4km (2.5 miles) this road merges with the C66 from Girona. Almost immediately you see the high peaks of the Pyrenees up ahead in the distance. Soon you reach Besalú (► 36–37); to explore this delightful town, park on the right, walk down to the riverbank and follow the signs to enter Besalú across the medieval Pont Vell.

Leaving Besalú, continue on the main road heading towards Olot.

This soon becomes the A26 road. When you see a tunnel ahead, take the exit on to the old N260 to Castellfollit de la Roca (► 98–99), perched on a ridge to your left.

Continue through this village and rejoin the A26. When the road ends, turn left towards Olot and keep left to skirt the city centre, following signs to Santa Pau.

Shortly after turning on to the Santa Pau road, you see the Can Serra car park and information centre on your left. If you have time, you could stop here and do the walk described on pages 106–107.

Continue on this winding road to Santa Pau (▶ 111). After exploring the village, return to the same road as it twists down to the plain, with lovely views all the way.

Eventually you arrive at Banyoles beside the lake.

Distance 76km (47 miles)
Time 2 hours plus stops along the way
Start/end point Banyoles ✚ 6E
Lunch Cal Sastre (€€) ✉ Placeta dels Balls 6, Santa Pau
☎ 972 68 04 21

Shopping for souvenirs

Agadi

A wide range of good-quality shoes at reasonable prices, for which Spain is renowned.

✉ Carrer Argentins 14, Girona ☎ 972 22 64 46

L'Artesanat

A great selection of colourful ceramics and decorative items for the home, as well as locally produced liqueurs.

✉ Carrer de la Forca 21, Girona ☎ No phone

Avelli

One of the largest pottery shops in La Bisbal, with a huge selection in all shapes and sizes.

✉ Carrer l'Aigüeta 60–68, La Bisbal ☎ 972 64 06 02

La Bisbal d'Art

Ceramics produced by local potters from the nearby village of Corca.

✉ Carrer l'Aigüeta 146, La Bisbal ☎ 972 64 32 32

La Botiga

Pottery and gift shop with some very attractive pieces on offer.

✉ Carrer l'Aigüeta 32, La Bisbal ☎ 972 64 18 02

Cal Ramón

Wonderfully fresh local *botifarras*, a type of pork sausage for which Vic is famous, plus good cheeses and other delicious local products.

✉ Place del Pes 5, Vic ☎ 938 86 11 05

Disennium

Striking dresses and fashions created by designers worldwide. Beautifully crafted jewellery and imaginative gifts of all kinds.

✉ Monturiol 4. Figueres ☎ 972 50 37 08

Estevez
Ladies and menswear, plus a good range of quality leather and suede handbags, belts and suitcases.

✉ Rambla 25, Figueres ☎ 972 50 01 45 and ✉ Girona 1, Figueres ☎ 972 67 21 89

Santa & Clara
A beautiful range of artistic goods, paintings, prints, medieval manuscripts, handmade glassware and home-made jams produced by the nuns from local convents. All very stylish and tasteful.

✉ Calle Forca, Girona ☎ 972 22 34 90a

Sclop
A new store with a good selection of top brand names offering exciting modern shoe designs.

✉ 1 Placa Major, La Bisbal ☎ 972 645460

Best beaches

- Blanes (➤ 158–159)

- Empúriabrava (➤ 139)

- L'Estartit (➤ 99)

- Lloret de Mar (➤ 162–165)

Places to take the children

Aquabrava

Waterslides, beaches and the biggest wave pool in Europe are among the attractions on offer.

✉ Carretera de Cadaqués, Roses ☎ 972 25 43 44; www.aquabrava.com
🕓 Jun–12 Sep daily 10–6:30 🚌 Free bus from Roses and Empúriabrava

Aquadiver

Children will love the wave machines, zigzagging toboggans, safe white-water rapids and the "kamikaze" free-fall ride at Aquadiver.

✉ Carretera Circumval.lació, Platja d'Aro ☎ 972 82 82 83;
www.aquadiver.com 🕓 Jun–Sep daily 10–6 (Jul–Aug 10–7) 🚌 Free bus from Platja d'Aro, Palamós and Sant Feliu de Guíxols

Butterfly Park Empuriabrava

This tropical rain forest, recreated in a large greenhouse, offers a magical world of colourful butterflies and exotic birds.

✉ Carretera Castelló–Empúriabrava ☎ 972 45 07 61; www.butterflypark.es
🕓 Apr–Oct daily 10–one hour before dusk

Gnomo Park

Little children will love this "gnome theme park", which offers mini-golf, an adventure playground, train rides, a woodland trail – and gnomes!

✉ Carretera Blanes–Lloret ☎ 972 36 80 80; www.gnomo-park.com 🕓 Easter–Oct Tue–Sun 11–9; Nov–Easter Sat–Sun 11–9

Magic Park

Funfair and indoor play area with roller-skating, a miniature boating lake, inflatable toys, dodgem cars, a carousel, video games and a soft play area for younger children. There is another Magic Park in Lloret de Mar.

✉ Avinguda S'Agaró 86, Platja d'Aro ☎ 972 81 78 64 🕐 Daily 10am–1am

Marineland

Aquatic park with dolphin and sea lion shows and a small zoo with penguins and seals. Thrill rides include the Black Hole, Boomerang, Kamikaze and Twister. Separate pools and rides for the under-6s; picnic area among the pine trees.

✉ Carretera Malgrat a Palafolls, near Blanes ☎ 937 65 48 02; www.marineland.es 🕐 May–Sep daily 10–6 (Jul–Aug 10–7) 🚌 Free bus from Blanes, Lloret de Mar and Tossa de Mar

The Nautilus Adventure

Children will enjoy any boat trip on the Costa Brava, but this one travels out to the Medes Islands in boats with submerged cabins, allowing you to observe the fish swimming along the seabed.

✉ Passeig Marítim 23, L'Estartit ☎ 972 75 14 89 🕐 Departures several times a day in summer and at winter weekends, depending on the weather

Parc Animal de Sobrestany

Wildlife park with deer, bison, wild boar, ostriches and Pyrenean sheep. There is a walking trail and a driving tour where you are given a bag of feed for the animals.

✉ Camí de Sobrestany, between Torroella de Montgrí and L'Escala ☎ 972 78 84 94 🕐 Daily 9–8 summer, 10–6 winter

Water World

Pools, slides and the Water Mountain, where you can take a big-dipping roller-coaster ride.

✉ Carretera Vidreres, Lloret de Mar ☎ 972 36 86 13; www.waterworld.es 🕐 May–Sep daily 10–6 (Jul–Aug 10–7:30) 🚌 Free bus from Blanes, Lloret de Mar and Tossa de Mar

Great coastal views

Cap de Creus (➤ 136)

Cap Roig, Calella de Palafrugell
(➤ 96–97)

Cap de Sant Sebastià, Llafranc
(➤ 101)

Castell de Begur, Begur (➤ 94)

Castell del Montgrí, Torroella de
Montgrí (➤ 113)

Castell de Sant Joan, Blanes
(➤ 159)

Castell de Sant Salvador, above
Monestir de Sant Pere de Rodes
(➤ 47)

Ermita de Sant Elm, Sant Feliu
de Guíxols (➤ 168)

Puig Rom, Roses (➤ 51)

**Tossa de Mar to Sant Feliu de
Guíxols** – views from the
belvederes along the coastal
corniche (➤ 54–55)

Golf courses

Club de Golf d'Aro – Mas Nou
27 holes, par 72. Attractive course surrounded by olive, pine, cork and oak trees.
✉ Urbanizacion Mas Nou s/n, Platja d'Aro ☎ 972 82 69 00; www.golfdaro.com

Club de Golf Costa Brava
18 holes, par 70. Near the beach resorts of Platja d'Aro and Sant Feliu de Guíxols, with two rounds – one more technical, the other more relaxing.
✉ Urbanizacion Golf Costa Brava "La Masia", Santa Cristina d'Aro ☎ 972 83 71 50; www.golfcostabrava.com

Empordà Golf Resort
36 holes, par 71 and 72. Prestigious course, with two rounds: Empordà links and Empordà forest.
✉ Carretera de Torroella a Palafrugell s/n, Gualta ☎ 972 76 04 50; www.empordagolf.com

Golf Girona
18 holes, par 72. High-quality course.
✉ Sant Julià de Ramis, 7km (4 miles) from Girona ☎ 972 17 16 41; www.golfgirona.com

Golf Peralada
18 holes, par 71. Magnificent location just outside the medieval village of Peralada.
✉ Avinguda Rocaberti s/n, Peralada ☎ 972 53 82 87; www.golfperalada.com

Golf Platja de Pals
18 holes, par 73. Opened in 1963, this is the oldest course on the Costa Brava.
✉ Cami del Golf 64, Pals ☎ 972 66 77 39; www.golfplatjadepals.com

Golf Serres de Pals
18 holes, par 72. Attractive course set among hills and pine
forests, with fairways edged by lakes.
✉ Avinguda Arenales de Mar s/n, Pals ☎ 972 63 73 75;
www.golfserresdepals.com

Mas Pages Golf
18 holes, par 54. Skill is required to take on this course,
surrounded by a shady forest.
✉ Mas Pages s/n, Sant Esteve de Guialbes ☎ 972 56 10 01;
www.maspages,com

PGA Golf de Catalunya
36 holes, par 72. Hosting some major international competitions,
this has two courses – one for more advanced golfers and an
easier one for players of all levels.
✉ Carretera N-11, Km 701, Caldes de Malavella ☎ 972 47 25 77;
www.pgacatalunya.com

Torremirona Golf Club
18 holes, par 72. Two rounds, one more technical and one to suit
golfers of all levels.
✉ Carretera Figueres–Olot ☎ 972 55 37 37; www.torremirona.com

Best small towns and villages

Begur: a pretty hilltop town crowned by a ruined castle (➤ 94)

Besalú: a beautifully restored historic capital, preserved as an open-air museum (➤ 36–37)

Cadaqués: this chic Catalan fishing village has become a shrine to Salvador Dalí (➤ 38–39)

Calella de Palafrugell: an enjoyable, old-style seaside resort with restaurants on the beach (➤ 96–97)

Castelló d'Empúries: an unassuming country town with a magnificent parish church (➤ 138–139)

Pals: a showpiece village of Gothic and medieval architecture
(► 108)

Peratallada: a fortified medieval village with stone bridges,
archways and cobbled streets (► 108)

Sant Pere Pescador: a laid-back riverside town with a splendid
unspoiled beach (► 146–147)

Santa Pau: a fortified village at the heart of the volcanic Garrotxa
region (► 111)

Torroella de Montgrí: an attractive market town in the shadow
of a 13th-century castle (► 112–113)

Music festivals

Cadaqués
International Festival of Arts and Music – both classical and contemporary, in August.
☎ 972 25 83 15

Calella de Palafrugell
A festival of *havaneres* is held on the beach on the first weekend in July, and a music festival takes place in the gardens of Cap Roig throughout July and August (➤ 96–97). There are also festivals of *havaneres* in the neighbouring resorts of Llafranc (➤ 101) and Tamariu (➤ 112).
☎ 972 61 44 75 (information); 972 44 77 55 (ticket sales)

Castelló d'Empúries
The cathedral is the venue for a music festival in August, plus a one-day festival featuring minstrels and traditional Catalan songs held on 11 September.
☎ 972 15 62 33

Girona
An annual music festival is held in Girona in July, and concerts with prestigious performers are held throughout the year in the Auditori Girona.
☎ 872 08 07 09

Olot
The biggest *sardana* festival in Catalonia takes places here on the second Sunday

in July, with participants from all over the region coming to perform this traditional dance.
☎ 972 26 01 41

Palafrugell
The Costa Brava Jazz Festival is held at various places in the town in October, with the main venue being the Teatro Municipal.
☎ 972 30 02 28

Peralada
Evening concerts are held in July and August in the Renaissance castle, with performances by top international artists.
☎ 972 53 82 92

Sant Feliu de Guíxols
One of the Costa Brava's foremost festivals takes place during July and August in the parish church of La Madre de Dios, with performances by internationally acclaimed musicians.
☎ 972 82 00 51

Torroella de Montgrí
This International Music Festival, one of the most prominent in Europe, is held in the main square and the Gothic church of Sant Genis in July and August, with performances of both classical music and jazz.
☎ 972 76 10 98

Exploring

When tourists started visiting Spain in the 1950s, it was to the Costa Brava that they came. Other, bigger costas followed, but it was this small corner near the French border that led the way. Fishing villages were transformed almost overnight into high-rise resorts; the face of the coastline changed more in a generation than in the previous thousand years. The Costa Brava virtually invented the sun-and-sea holiday.

Yet those rocky creeks still exist. There are villas climbing up the hillsides now, but this is still recognizable as Agulló's Wild Coast. There are areas of unspoiled marshland, Greek and Roman ruins and long, sandy beaches with not a hotel in sight. The main town, Girona, has a charming, medieval heart, and further inland are solid Catalan towns like Olot and Vic.

The Costa Brava is changing its image – no longer cheap and cheerful, but chic, confident and cool.

Girona and Central Costa Brava

The craggy coastline of cliffs, coves and cork woods at the heart of the Costa Brava epitomizes the nature of the "Wild Coast". Tourism has arrived here, but slowly – there are few high-rise hotels, and the villas on the hillsides are mostly second homes for the people of Barcelona. The tranquil resorts around Begur and Palafrugell, with their sandy beaches and shimmering bays, are some of the most relaxing places on the entire Catalan coast.

Girona □

Inland, towns like Besalú and Pals have been restored to their medieval splendour, while the Garrotxa region of sleeping volcanoes around Olot makes for an interesting day out. There are historic castles and monasteries to be explored, and Girona, the provincial capital, is one of the most pleasing cities in Spain. This region also offers a variety of walks along stunning coastal routes or signposted trails leading through the forests and hills of the hinterland.

GIRONA

The capital of the Costa Brava region was founded by the Romans on the site of an Iberian settlement in the 1st century BC. Over the years it has been subject to numerous invasions, including Charlemagne in 785 and Napoleon in 1809. The city you see today consists of a medieval centre built on top of the Roman foundations, and an expanding new town across the Onyar River.

You can still make out traces of the old Roman city. Carrer de la Força, the cobbled street at the heart of the Jewish quarter, was once part of the Roman Via Augusta, a continental highway linking Rome to southern Spain. The Sobreportes arch at the foot of the cathedral steps is built over one of the old Roman entrances to the city. The statue of the Virgin of Good Death standing in a niche above the arch is a reminder that in later times prisoners were led through this gate to their execution.

But modern Girona is about more than ancient monuments. It's a thriving university city and a lively provincial capital. The city has been called Barcelona's little sister. It has all the style of the Catalan capital, but is more intimate and approachable.

➕ 19H

ℹ️ Carrer Joan Maragall 2, tel: 872 97 59 75

Banys Àrabs

The so-called Arab Baths are a 13th-century Romanesque creation, based on an earlier Moorish design and influenced by Roman styles. They are one of the best preserved medieval bathhouses in Spain. The most impressive room is the apodyterium or changing-room, with an octagonal pool at its centre beneath a domed skylight supported by eight columns. From here you can walk through the frigidarium (cold chamber) and tepidarium (warm bath) to reach the caldarium, an early sauna with underground heating. The baths regularly host exhibitions.

➕ *Girona 7b* ✉️ Carrer del Rei Ferran el Catòlic 🕐 Apr–Sep Mon–Sat 10–7, Sun 10–2; Oct–May daily 10–2 ✋ Inexpensive

Call Jueu

For six centuries until their expulsion in 1492, Girona was home to one of the largest Jewish communities in Spain. At one time up to 1,000 Jews lived in the area around Carrer de la Força, where there were three synagogues, a Jewish school, a ritual bath and a Jewish butcher.

At the centre of the Jewish ghetto is the Centre Bonastruc Ça Porta. This cultural centre with its Jewish museum is named after the celebrated founder of the Cabbalist school of Judaism, also known as Rabbi Nahmánides, who was born in Girona in 1194. Cabbalism is a secret system of mysticism, metaphysics and mathematics that claims to read hidden messages into the scriptures. The fascinating little **Museu d'Història dels Jueus** tells the tragic story of Catalonia's Jews, who were persecuted for 300 years before being finally driven out. Centuries later, this small centre in Girona is providing a focus for the renaissance of Jewish Spain.

✚ *Girona 7c* 🍽 El Pou del Call, Carrer de la Força 14 (€€)

Museu d'Història dels Jueus

✉ Carrer de la Força 8 ☎ 972 21 67 61 🕐 Jun–Oct Mon–Sat 10–8; Nov–May Mon–Sat 10–6, Sun 10–5 ✋ Inexpensive

Catedral

Girona's cathedral is one of the great churches of Spain. Begun in 1312 on the site of an earlier church (and before that a mosque), it has evolved over the succeeding centuries into a triumph of different architectural styles, coming together to create a unifying and satisfying whole.

The best way to approach the cathedral is via the huge rococo staircase leading up to its Renaissance facade, an exquisite piece of stone carving with floral reliefs and sculptures of saints supporting the central rose window. Inside, the cathedral is dominated by its single Gothic nave, at 23m (75ft) the widest in Europe. Other features to look out for include the 11th-century alabaster altarpiece (a remnant of the earlier church) and the embossed silver canopy above the high altar.

The Treasury contains an illustrated 10th-century manuscript of the *Beatus*, or Commentary on the Apocalypse and the 11th-century *Tapestry of the Creation*. The ticket also gives access to the 12th-century Romanesque cloisters, with a view of the original bell tower, Torre de Carlemany, skilfully incorporated into the 14th-century Gothic design.

www.catedralgirona.org

✚ *Girona 7b* ✉ Plaça de la Catedral ☎ 972 21 44 26 🕓 Apr–Oct daily 10–8; Nov–Mar 10–7 ✋ Moderate (free on Sun). Ticket allows entry to the museum and cloisters. Audio-guide is also included in the price of the ticket

❓ Access through the main door is for services only; visitors enter through the side door

a walk around Girona Old Town

This walk is best done during the early evening, when the citizens of Girona take their *passeig* along the Rambla.

Start at Pont de Pedra, the stone bridge to the north of Plaça de Catalunya. Cross this bridge to reach the old town and continue into the arcaded Plaça del Vi. Turn left and cross the square to reach Carrer dels Ciutadans.

At this point you could take one of the narrow alleys to your left to explore the medieval streets of the guilds (► 45).

Carrer dels Ciutadans leads into Plaça de l'Oli. Turn right to climb the steps towards the church of Sant Martí. Halfway up the steps, fork left beneath the arch formed by the facade of Palau dels Agullana, a handsome Gothic mansion. Continue climbing to reach Plaça Sant Domènec, dominated by its old university. Turn left to leave the square, then left again along Carrer dels Alemanys into Carrer Bellmirall.

Turn right and cross Plaça dels Lledoners to reach the cathedral's southern door. After visiting the cathedral, walk down the flight of steps beneath its main facade into Plaça de la Catedral.

Turn left along Carrer de la Força. This road, and the steep, dark alleys to its left, form the heart of the atmospheric Jewish quarter (► 84). Reaching a small square, descend the steps to your right, leading to Carrer de l'Argenteria.

This smart shopping street leads into the Rambla (➤ 92), where you can end your walk with *tapas* and a drink beneath the arches.

Distance 2km (1.2 miles)
Time 1 hour
Start/end point Pont de Pedra 🚉 *Girona 6d* 🚌 1km (0.5 miles) from bus and railway stations
Tapas Café l'Arcada (€), Rambla de l'Libertat 38, tel: 972 21 22 77

Eixample

Most visitors to Girona spend all their time in the old town to the east of the River Onyar, but the Eixample ("extension"), on the other side of the river, is where most people live and work. Plaça de la Independència, where the old town meets the new, is a pleasant 19th-century arcaded square lined with restaurants, cafes and bars. The monument at the centre is to the defenders of Girona, under siege from Napoleon's troops in 1809. A short walk fleads to the Parc de la Devesa, the city's playground and the largest urban park in Catalonia. Also near here is the **Museu del Cinema,** a fascinating collection of old cameras and cinematographic instruments.

Much of the new town was built in the early years of the 20th century, when the Modernist architectural movement was at its peak. Rafael Masó, born in Girona in 1880, was one of the leading figures in the movement. His Casa Teixidor, with its green ceramic lantern, can be seen on Carrer Santa Eugènia near the station. Designed as a warehouse with flats above, it is now a college of architecture.

🕂 *Girona 5c* 🍴 Massana (€€), Bonastruc de Porta 10–12 🚌 Girona bus station is in this area 🚉 Girona station

Museu del Cinema
✉ Carrer Sèquia 1 ☎ 972 41 27 77 🕓 May–Sep Tue–Sun 10–8; Oct–Apr Tue–Fri 10–6, Sat 10–8, Sun 11–3 ✋ Moderate

Església de Sant Feliu
Girona's second church is easily recognized by its broken spire, damaged by lightning in 1581 and never repaired. It's an essential feature of the skyline when seen from the Onyar river. Built over the tomb of Feliu of Africa, a 4th-century Bishop of Girona, the church is a mix of architectural styles, from Romanesque to Gothic to baroque. Interesting features include the Roman sarcophagi, both pagan and Christian, built into the sanctuary walls, and the neoclassical chapel of Sant Narcís, with its marble walls and painted ceiling.

🕂 *Girona 6b* ✉ Plaça de Sant Feliu ☎ 972 41 27 20 🕓 Mon–Sat 10–2, 5–7, Sun 10–2 ✋ Free

Museu Arqueològic

This museum, in the 12th-century
Romanesque monastery of Sant Pere
de Galligants, contains an interesting
collection of artefacts, from prehistoric
to medieval times. Among the finds are
Roman pottery and mosaics from
Empúries (► 42–43) and three Roman
milestones indicating the distance to
Gerunda – the Roman name for the
city. The cloister is notable for its
beautifully sculpted capitals of
mythological and biblical figures. The
gardens around the back, with their
shady fountains and views of the
cathedral, would make a lovely spot for
a siesta or a picnic.

➕ Girona 7b ✉ Plaça de Santa Llúcia s/n
☎ 972 20 26 32 🕔 Jun–Sep Tue–Fri
10:30–1:30, 4–7, Sat–Sun 10–2; Oct–May
Tue–Fri 10–2, 4–6, Sat–Sun 10–2
✋ Inexpensive

Museu d'Art

This museum, housed in the former
episcopal palace, contains a large
collection of Catalan art, from
Romanesque to contemporary. Among
the exhibits are the 10th-century
portable altar from the monastery of
Sant Pere de Rodes (► 46–47), the
14th-century stencils used to design
stained-glass windows for Girona's
cathedral, and the scenes of 20th-

century Girona by the Catalan artist Santiago Rusinyol and the Polish painter Mela Mutter.

✚ *Girona 7c* ✉ Pujada de la Catedral 12 ☎ 972 20 38 34 ◉ Mar–Sep Tue–Sat 10–7, Sun 10–2; Oct–Feb Tue–Sat 10–6, Sun 10–2 👋 Inexpensive

Museu d'Història de la Ciutat

The city museum, in the former Capuchin monastery of Sant Antoni, details the history of Girona from prehistoric times to today. Among the more unusual exhibits, the ground-floor display on industrial history features an old petrol pump, wireless sets and an early computer. Upstairs, there is a room devoted to the development of the *sardana* dance. The cemetery of the original convent is preserved just inside the entrance, with niches on the walls designed for mummified corpses.

✚ *Girona 6c* ✉ Carrer de la Força 27 ☎ 972 22 22 29 ◉ Tue–Sat 10–2, 5–7, Sun 10–2 👋 Inexpensive

Passeig de les Muralles

This walkway, along the medieval ramparts, offers marvellous views over the city. It begins near Plaça de Catalunya and continues past the convent and university of Sant Domènec to the ruined watchtower, Torre Gironella. For the best views, climb onto some of the newly restored towers, from where the distant peaks of the Pyrenees are visible on a clear day. The walk ends at Passeig Arqueològic, a series of attractively landscaped gardens between the cathedral and the River Galligants.

✚ *Girona 8d* ◉ Daily 8am–10pm 👋 Free

Rambla and Riu Onyar

The Rambla beside the River Onyar is the hub of Girona's social life, and the best place to see it all is from one of the cafes beneath the vaulted arches. The Pont de Pedra, the stone bridge at the top of the Rambla, looks down over the river, with its iron and wooden bridges and brightly painted tenement houses backing on to the water. One of the bridges, the Pont de les Peixateries, cuts directly through the houses and on to the Rambla. It was built for the city by the French firm of Eiffel and Company, creators of the famous tower in Paris.

✚ *Girona 6d* 🍴 L'Arcada (€€), Rambla de la Llibertad 38 ❓ Flower market Sat; Festa de Sant Jordi; book and flower market 23 Apr; flower festival May

Central Costa Brava

AIGUABLAVA

It was here, in 1908, that the journalist Ferran Agulló first coined the term *costa brava*, and the rocky coves around Begur retain much of their ruggedness today. Of course they have now been discovered by tourists, and luxury urbanizations are creeping up the hillsides, but out of season you can still have pine-fringed cliffs, golden sand and sparkling turquoise bays (Aiguablava means blue water) to yourself. The bay at Aiguablava is dominated, unusually, by an ugly white *parador*, a state-run hotel built on the cliffs to take advantage of the view. Across the bay is the chic resort of Fornells, little more than a marina, a smart hotel and a pair of tiny beaches. North of here are more small coves – Sa Riera, with views over the Medes islands, and Aiguafreda and Sa Tuna, linked by a footpath cut into the rock.

✚ 23H ⭐ Restaurants and bars at Aiguablava, Sa Riera and Sa Tuna (€€–€€€) 🚌 From Begur to Aiguablava, Aiguafreda and Fornells in summer

BANYOLES

The capital of the Pla de l'Estany county makes a pleasant place to while away a summer afternoon. The main square, Plaça Major, is a perfect example of the genre, with three- and four-storey houses climbing above the ground-floor arcades. Just outside Banyoles is a lake, fed by an underground spring, where the 1992 Olympic rowing contests and the 2004 World Championships were held. You can swim, fish, rent a rowing boat or walk the 8km (5 miles) around the lake's shore. The jawbone of a pre-Neanderthal man, at least 100,000 years old, was discovered in 1887. A copy is kept in the **Museu Arqueològic,** in the 14th-century almshouses.

➕ 6E 🍴 La Cisterna (€€), Carrer Paissos Catalans 36 🚌 From Besalú, Girona and Olot

ℹ️ Plaça Major 38, tel: 972 57 55 73

Museu Arqueològic

✉️ Plaça de la Font 11 ☎️ 972 57 23 61 🕐 Jul–Aug Tue–Sat 10:30–1:30, 4–7:30, Sun 10:30–2; Sep–Jun Tue–Sat 10:30–1:30, 4–6:30, Sun 10:30–2 ✋ Inexpensive

BEGUR

This hilltop town with a ruined 15th-century castle makes a good base for exploring the rocky coves around Aiguablava (➤ 93). Narrow streets fan out from the church square, and you can climb to the castle for great views stretching north along the coastline as far as the Bay of Roses. Begur has grown in popularity and a rash of new holiday villas and apartments has contributed to a sense of urban sprawl, with fears that the medieval centre could be overwhelmed by development. Nevertheless, it remains a quiet and peaceful place, popular with Catalan weekenders.

➕ 23H 🍴 Aiguablava (€€, ➤ 58) 🚌 From Girona and Palafrugell

❓ Market on Wed

BESALÚ

Best places to see, ➤ 36–37.

LA BISBAL D'EMPORDÀ

La Bisbal is best known as the centre of the Catalan ceramics industry. Its most abiding image – and the only one that many visitors see – is of the dozens of pottery shops lining Carrer de l'Aigüeta on the Girona road. There are good bargains to be had if you shop around, from simple glazed terracotta pots to innovative local designs. A twin-arched bridge, Pont Vell, leads over the River Daró into the centre of the old town, which comes alive each Friday with one of the region's busiest markets. Wander the narrow lanes and you keep coming across little surprises – a Gothic archway here, a fountain there, a shop selling hand-crafted wooden chairs or a shrine to the Virgin of Montserrat set high into a wall. The Romanesque bishops' palace, on the old town square, is a reminder that this quiet county town was once the seat of the bishops of Girona.

✚ 21H 🍴 Castell d'Empordà (€€€), Carretera del Castell d'Empordà s/n
🚌 From Girona and Palafrugell ❓ Market on Fri
ℹ️ Plaça del Castell, tel: 972 64 51 66

CALELLA DE PALAFRUGELL

This delightful resort consists of a series of coarse, sandy beaches strung out beneath an old fishing village. The village now includes a few whitewashed holiday villas, but it has lost none of its original

charm. You can still see working fishermen here, and fishing boats on the sand add a splash of colour to the scene. The people of Palafrugell and beyond head to Calella at weekends to eat at the waterfront seafood restaurants, while their children play on the beach.

Calella de Palafrugell is the setting for one of the Costa Brava's more unusual festivals each July, when popular musicians gather to sing *havaneres* on the beach. These melancholy sea shanties, brought back from Cuba by Spanish sailors and rooted in the Creole music of the Caribbean, have been sung in the fishermen's taverns for at least 100 years. They are best enjoyed while drinking *cremat*, a local concoction of coffee, rum and cinnamon, which is served flambéed.

A cliff path from Calella leads around to the next bay at Llafranc (➤ 101). At the other end of the village, high above the bay, is the **Jardí Botànic de Cap Roig,** a beautiful garden laid out in 1927 by a White Russian emigré, Colonel Nicolai Woevodsky, and his English wife, Dorothy Webster. There are cypress, cork oak and mimosa trees, and hundreds of Mediterranean plants, tall cedars and pine trees, bent by the wind and leaning towards the sea as if paying homage to the Mediterranean.

➕ 23H 🍴 Can Palet (€€, ➤ 120) 🚌 From Palafrugell ❓ Festival of *havaneres*, first Sat in Jul

ℹ️ Carrer de les Voltes 6, tel: 972 61 44 75

Jardí Botànic de Cap Roig

✉️ Cap Roig, 4km (2.5 miles) from village ☎ 972 61 45 82 🕐 Mar–Jun, Sep daily 9–8; Oct–Dec 9–6; Jan–Feb Sat–Sun 9–6; Jul–Aug days of concerts 9–2

👐 Moderate ❓ Cap Roig Gardens Festival held each Jul and Aug

CASTELL GALA DALÍ
Best places to see, ➤ 40–41.

CASTELLFOLLIT DE LA ROCA
Spectacularly perched on a 1km-long (0.6-mile) basalt promontory, carved out by the River Fluvià, this village looks for all the world as if it is about to fall off the cliff. The best view is from below, as you approach Castellfollit on the road from Besalú. At night, the cliff is floodlit and you can pick out the different geological layers in the

rock. The narrow streets of the village, their houses built from volcanic stone, converge by a church, where you can gaze 60m (195ft) down into the precipice below. Castellfollit is known for its almond biscuits and its pork sausages, and in the **Museu de l'Embotit** (Sausage Museum) you can taste the local products after looking at old-fashioned mincing machines and models of the *matança* or annual slaughter of pigs.

➕ 4D 🍴 Fonda Ca La Paula on main street (€) 🚌 From Besalú, Figueres, Girona and Olot

Museu de l'Embotit
✉ Carretera Girona 10 ☎ 972 29 44 63 🕐 Mon–Sat 9:30–1:30, 4–8, Sun 9:30–2, 4:30–8 👋 Free

L'ESTARTIT

What was once little more than a fishing harbour, serving the nearby town of Torroella de Montgrí (➤ 112–113), has grown into a bustling, modern holiday resort with a reputation for nightlife and a thriving watersports industry. The main attraction here is the beach, which stretches for 5km (3 miles) and is backed by a seafront promenade. This is a good resort for families with young children – the water is shallow, the sand shelves gently and a miniature train trundles along the seafront. Unlike some of the larger resorts to the south, L'Estartit virtually closes down in winter, when all the locals retreat to Torroella de Montgrí. A popular attraction in summer is a boat trip to the Medes Islands (➤ 100), 1km (0.5 miles) offshore.

➕ 11F 🍴 Felix (€€, ➤ 121) 🚌 From Girona and Torroella de Montgrí ⛴ Trips to Cadaqués and Palamós in summer

ℹ Passeig Marítim, tel: 972 75 19 10

ILLES MEDES

Seven rocky islets, a continuation of the Montgrí massif, harbour a rich diversity of plant and animal life in one of the most important nature reserves in the western Mediterranean. Local fishermen, banned from fishing in the area, feared for their livelihood; but the protection of the marine environment has been such a success that catches are up everywhere else as a result. Scuba divers come from all over Spain to swim among coral reefs and caves teeming with grouper, scorpion fish and spiny lobsters. Glass-bottomed boats leave regularly in summer from the harbour at L'Estartit (➤ 99); some trips include the opportunity to go snorkelling. There are strict regulations about fishing, boating and night diving in the

protected area, and it is essential to check with the authorities at the harbour in L'Estartit. In the past the islands were used as a pirate hideout and a French military prison, but nowadays they are uninhabited – apart from the seabirds, especially the thousands of yellow-legged gulls, who breed here between March and May each year.

🚩 11F 🛥 Trips from L'Estartit in summer and occasionally on winter weekends

ℹ Passeig Marítim, tel: 972 75 19 10

LLAFRANC

Pine trees shade a beachfront promenade and yachts flutter in the small marina beside a perfect bay, where tamarisks grow out of the rocks around an arc of fine sand. Llafranc's development is restrained and few of the buildings are more than two or three storeys high. A coastal path leads to Calella de Palafrugell (➤ 96–97), or you can walk or drive up to the lighthouse at Cap de Sant Sebastià for views back down over Llafranc.

✚ 23H 🍴 Restaurant El Far (€€–€€€), Platja de Llafranc s/n 🚌 From Palafrugell ❓ Festival of *havaneres* on the beach, first Sat in Aug
ℹ Carrer Roger de Llúria, tel: 972 30 50 08

OLOT

The capital of the Garrotxa region is a truly Catalan town, which manages to be both industrious and stylish, conservative at heart with a radical edge. The people of Olot have a strong sense of Catalan identity: you are unlikely to hear anyone speaking Spanish. This Catalan spirit is openly displayed at the town's two biggest festivals – the *Aplec de la Sardana*, on the second Sunday in July, when visitors come from all over Catalonia to perform the *sardana* dance; and the *Festa de la Tura*, on 8 September, when figures of giants and hobby horses parade through the streets.

Olot was a centre of textile production, and an art school was opened here in the 18th century. A century later, one of its pupils, Joaquim Vayreda, helped to found the Olot School of Art. The romantic scenes of rural life produced by these early Catalan impressionists were influenced by the European trends of the time, yet rooted in the Garrotxa landscape of volcanic hills.

The smart shopping streets of the old town around the Plaça Major lead to the neoclassical parish church of Sant Esteve. Near here is the start of the Rambla, also named Passeig Miquel Blay, after a well-known Olot sculptor. This delightful promenade, with coffee tables beneath the trees, contains some unusual Modernist architecture, as well as the 19th-century Teatre Principal. The Rambla is also the venue for Olot's lively market, which takes place on Monday mornings.

✠ 3E

ℹ Carrer del'Hospici 8, tel: 972 26 01 41

Casal dels Volcans

The Garrotxa region around Olot has been at the centre of volcanic activity for hundreds of thousands of years. Although the most recent eruption was more than 11,000 years ago, the volcanoes are still considered dormant. Nor are volcanoes the only threat. A major earthquake struck the city in 1427, and there were tremors at nearby Besalú as recently as 1988. This museum, in the House of Volcanoes inside the botanic gardens at Parc Nou, explores the history and geology of the region, and its fauna and flora. The information centre for the Garrotxa natural park, in an office above the museum, is a good place to pick up leaflets about the area and walking maps and guides.

A waymarked walk (No 17) from the museum leads to the Volcà de Montsacopa, a typical volcano just north of the town centre. You can get there just as easily by following the signs from the Museu Comarcal, from where it will take around 20 minutes to reach the crater. Pass market gardens on the lower slopes, then walk uphill through an avenue of plane trees lined with Stations of the Cross. From the chapel of Sant Francesc, on the summit, there are marvellous views back down over Olot's rooftops and over the surrounding landscape, carved out by volcanic activity. You can walk right around the rim of the crater, or follow the path down to its floor. Another path leads to the crater of Volcà de la Garrinada, 500m (550yds) away.

✉ Avinguda de Santa Coloma (1km/0.6 miles from town)
☎ 972 26 67 62 🕐 Tue–Fri 10–2, 3–6, Sat 10–2, 4–7,
Sun 10–2 👣 Inexpensive 🍴 Cafe (€)

Museu Comarcal de la Garrotxa

An 18th-century hospice houses this county
museum of Garrotxa, with the most important
collection of work from the Olot School of Art.
Key figures in the movement were Josep Berga
i Boix (1837–1914) and Joaquim Vayreda
(1843–94). Many of Vayreda's paintings of rural
life are on display. The Modernist sculptor Miquel
Blay was also influenced by the Olot School;
among his works is a portrait of Berga i Boix.
More modern work includes nudes by sculptor
Josep Clarà, a pupil of Berga i Boix. The museum
also includes displays on Olot's traditional
industries – bell-making, clog-making, textiles
and religious statuary.

✉ Carrer de l'Hospici 8 ☎ 972 27 11 66 🕐 Jul–Sep
Tue–Sat 11–2, 4–7, Sun 11–2; Oct–Jun Tue–Fri 10–1,
3–6, Sat 11–2, 4–7, Sun 11–2 👣 Inexpensive
❓ Combined entry ticket available with Casal dels
Volcans and Museu dels Sants

Museu dels Sants d'Olot

Olot's saints form an integral part of the town's
history and a number of workshops produce
religious images. The museum of saints serves
not only as a showcase of Olot's cultural
heritage, but also as a means to encourage this
particular craft.

✉ Carrer Joaquim Vayreda 9 ☎ 972 26 67 91 🕐 Tue–Fri
10–1, 3–6, Sat 10–1, 4–7, Sun 11–2 👣 Inexpensive

a walk near Olot

This easy-to-follow walk provides an excellent introduction to the volcanic landscape around Olot and takes in three of its best-known features.

Start at the Can Serra car park, 5km (3 miles) out of Olot on the Santa Pau road. There is an information centre here where you can pick up a map of the walk. Take the underpass beneath the main road and descend the steps into the Fageda d'en Jordà beech wood.

The entire walk is waymarked with the symbol of two walkers on a red background accompanied by the number 1. The walk continues through this shady wood, joining a paved road to emerge beside a yoghurt factory before climbing sharply to the 11th-century church of Sant Miquel de Sacot.

Follow the waymarks. A short drop followed by a steep climb leads to the summit of the Santa Margarida volcano, from where an optional circular path heads down into the crater, with a small hermitage at its centre.

The path now descends to the main road, passing a farm where you can buy drinks and snacks.

Cross the road and take the lane that leads past the Santa Margarida restaurant, skirting the Volcà del Croscat. Until recently this volcano was quarried for its stone, and another optional path (No 15) leads to the scarred cliff-face to see the dramatic effects of the quarrying.

Continue around this volcano, and return through more beech woods to Can Serra.

Distance 10km (6 miles) plus optional extras
Time 3–4 hours
Start/end point Can Serra
Lunch Restaurant Santa Margarida (€), opposite Lava campsite on the GI524, tel: 972 68 02 70; closed May

PALAFRUGELL

A growing community of British expatriates has been attracted to this busy market town on the edge of the Lower Empordà plain, drawn to its down-to-earth Catalan atmosphere and the excellent beaches. It was once an important centre of cork production, and the Museu del Suro (cork museum) has displays on the history of the cork industry, as well as a selection of artefacts made from cork. The best time to visit Palafrugell is on Sunday, when the streets fill with stalls for one of the region's liveliest markets.

🚌 23H 🍴 La Xicra (€€€, ➤ 123) 🚍 From Girona and nearby beaches
❓ Market on Sun; Spring Festival, Whit Sunday; annual festival, 19–21 Jul
ℹ️ Carrer Carrilet 2, tel: 972 30 02 28

PALS

This walled village of Gothic stone houses around a 15th-century castle was abandoned in 1939 after the Spanish Civil War, but was lovingly restored after 1948. At times the village is too pretty for its own good – numerous galleries and pottery shops testify to its popularity with tourists. To appreciate it at its best you should come in the early morning or the evening, when the sunlight is at its most subtle and you can enjoy the alleys and archways without the crowds. The sandy beach of Platja de Pals, with its modern holiday facilities, is 5km (3 miles) away on the coast.

🚌 22G 🍴 Mas de Torrent (€€€, ➤ 123) 🚍 From Palafrugell
ℹ️ Plaça Major 7, tel: 972 63 73 80

PERATALLADA

A bridge leads across the original moat to this medieval village, (the name means hewn stone), and the cobbled alleyways are full of stone houses bearing ancient coats of arms. People travel for long distances at weekends to eat in Peratallada's restaurants, and to wander the back streets around the 11th-century castle.

🚌 22G 🍴 Can Bonay (€€, ➤ 123)
ℹ️ Carrer Unió 3, tel: 972 64 55 22

RIPOLL

Wilfred the Hairy, the first Count of Barcelona, used Ripoll as a base from which to unite the rival factions of the southern Pyrenees, following the reconquest of Catalonia from the Moors. He founded the **Monestir de Santa Maria** in 879 on the site of an earlier Visigothic church. During its golden age in the 11th and 12th centuries, the monastery ruled over an area stretching from Barcelona into modern France and became a great centre of European learning. Most of the church was destroyed by fire during the dissolution of the monasteries in 1835, but the great west portal survived. This is one of the jewels of Catalan Romanesque architecture, its pillars and arches covered in vivid reliefs of biblical stories, zodiac signs and scenes from agricultural life. The 12th-century cloisters of the monastery church have also survived, with expressive faces on the sculpted capitals. The nearby Museu Etnogràfic has everything from matchboxes and cowbells to Civil War posters gathered by a local historian.

✚ 1E (off map) 🍽 Recapolis (€€), Carretera Sant Joan 68 🚌 From Girona and Olot ❓ Market on Sat; wool festival,and farmer's wedding festival, May
ℹ️ Plaça de L'Abat s/n, tel: 972 70 23 51

Monestir de Santa Maria

✉ Plaça Abat Oliba 🕐 Daily 10–1, 3–7 ✋ Inexpensive

SANT JOAN DE LES ABADESSES

The convent here was established by Wilfred the Hairy as a gift
for his daughter Emma, whom he appointed the first abbess.
The 9th-century original has been replaced with a 12th-century
Romanesque church; its greatest treasure is its carved wooden
Calvary. Other sights in this attractive town, a good place to break
a journey between Ripoll and Olot, include a strangely pointed
bridge over the River Ter and the church of Sant Pol, with a tile
sculpture of *sardana* dancers among the ruins.

🚪 1D 🍴 Casa Rudes (€, ➤ 123)
🚌 From Ripoll ❓ Market
on Sun

SANTA PAU

The tourist capital of the
Garrotxa region has at its
heart a fortified medieval
enclave with a well-restored
baronial castle. The centre of
the village is closed to
traffic, so it is best to park

outside and walk in through the original gateway, Portal Nou. Plaça
Major, the main square, is as attractive as any in Catalonia, with
wooden balconies, stone arcades and the Romanesque church
of Santa Maria. The castle, first built in the 14th century, is in the
neighbouring square, Placeta dels Balls. A short walk from here
is the Mirador Portal del Mar, giving panoramic views over the
Garrotxa valleys and a distant glimpse of the sea. Santa Pau is an
excellent base for exploring this volcanic region – you can follow
numerous well-marked footpaths, hire a mountain-bike or a horse,
take a ride in a horse-drawn carriage or fly over the volcanoes in
a helicopter or a balloon.

🚪 4E 🍴 Cal Sastre (€€, ➤ 124) 🚌 Occasional buses from Olot and
Banyoles ❓ For balloon flights contact Vol de Coloms ☎ 972 68 02 55

TAMARIU

Named after the tamarisk trees that once surrounded its bay,
Tamariu is the smallest and prettiest of the three resorts on this
stretch of coastline near Palafrugell. In recent years it has become
decidedly chic, and many of the old fishermen's cottages have
been turned into holiday homes for Catalan families from Girona
and Barcelona. The main beach, a crescent of golden sand, is
backed by a wide pedestrian promenade lined with seafood
restaurants. A short walk around the headland to the north leads
to the rocky cove of Aiguaxellida, with its own small beach.

➕ 23H 🍴 Es Dofi (€€, ➤ 124) 🚌 From Palafrugell in summer ❓ Festival of
havaneres on the beach, first Sat in Sep

ℹ️ Carrer de la Riera, tel: 972 62 01 93

TORROELLA DE MONTGRÍ

This delightful town of Gothic palaces, courtyards and narrow
streets comes alive each Monday as the weekly market spills out
in all directions from the porticoed main square, Plaça de la Vila.
Stalls are piled high with local cheeses and sausages in this spot,
where the *sardana*, the modern Catalan folk dance, was danced
for the first time. The nearby **Can Quintana** cultural centre,

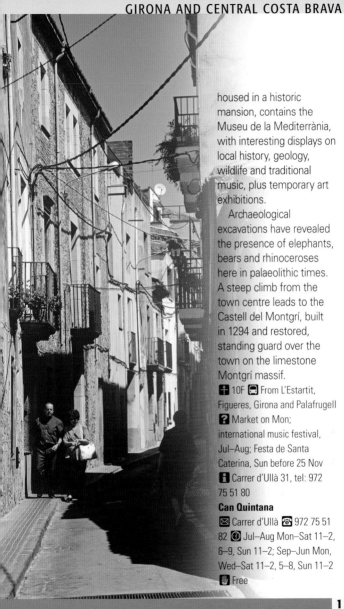

housed in a historic mansion, contains the Museu de la Mediterrània, with interesting displays on local history, geology, wildlife and traditional music, plus temporary art exhibitions.

Archaeological excavations have revealed the presence of elephants, bears and rhinoceroses here in palaeolithic times. A steep climb from the town centre leads to the Castell del Montgrí, built in 1294 and restored, standing guard over the town on the limestone Montgrí massif.

✚ 10F 🚌 From L'Estartit, Figueres, Girona and Palafrugell ❓ Market on Mon; international music festival, Jul–Aug; Festa de Santa Caterina, Sun before 25 Nov ℹ Carrer d'Ullà 31, tel: 972 75 51 80

Can Quintana

✉ Carrer d'Ullà ☎ 972 75 51 82 🕐 Jul–Aug Mon–Sat 11–2, 6–9, Sun 11–2; Sep–Jun Mon, Wed–Sat 11–2, 5–8, Sun 11–2 💷 Free

a walk from Tamariu

This walk begins with a short stretch of rocky coastline, before heading inland for the gentle climb to the summit of Puig Gruí (154m/505ft).

Start on the beach at Tamariu. From the southern end of the beach, near the car-parking area, cross to the smaller beach of Platja dels Liris and climb the steps, marked with red and white stripes, to join the GR92 coastal path.

Keep to the waymarks. You have to scramble across one rocky cove and climb around the next before levelling out on to a path running behind a stone wall.

At the next cove, climb for a few metres, then turn left through a grove of tamarisk trees. Continue to follow the red and white waymarks.

Eventually the path curves right, following the bend in the sea, then zigzags down to the pebble beach at the tiny cove of Cala Pedrosa.

Take the path directly behind the beach, climbing through the valley; at the top of this path turn right (leaving the GR92) to reach a road. Turn left along this road. After 50m (55yds), take the track on your right, just after a crossroads sign. The path is now marked with yellow and white stripes.

Passing an old well and a vineyard, you climb through a tamarisk wood, with occasional glimpses of the sea to your right, until you reach the summit of Puig Gruí.

Keep to the waymarks. The path turns right and drops steeply through the forest until it reaches a road with a wide circle. Turn right and continue on this road to return to Tamariu.

Distance 8km (5 miles)
Time 2.5 hours
Start/end point Tamariu 🚆 23H 🚌 From Palafrugell in summer
Lunch Es Dofí (€€, ➤ 124)

ULLASTRET

Archaeological excavations at Ullastret have revealed most of what we know about the ancient Iberian culture, which thrived here between the 6th and 2nd centuries BC. The Iberians were the first Spanish people to develop a written language; they learned pottery and metallurgy, and established towns and trading centres.

The Iberian settlement at Ullastret is the largest yet discovered in Catalonia. This fortified village was built on what was an island on a marshy lake, but is now at the centre of a fertile plain. Parts of the walls and the defensive towers remain, together with public buildings including cisterns, grain stores and a pair of temples to an unknown god. Most of the remains date from around the 3rd century BC; they were probably built over the foundations of earlier houses. The village was abandoned in the 2nd century BC, and remained deserted until excavations began in 1947.

A museum in the former chapel of Sant Andreu interprets the remains and contains finds from the excavations. There is a model of the site, and the displays describe the Iberian lifestyle (hunting, fishing, quarrying, metalwork), the development of money and of trading with the Greeks, and the rituals of cremation and child burial, which hint at the possibility of child sacrifice.

✚ 21G ✉ Puig de Sant Andreu ☎ 972 17 90 58 🕐 Easter and Jun–Sep Tue–Sun 10–8; Oct–May Tue–Sun 10–2, 3–6 ✋ Inexpensive (audio-guide costs extra)

HOTELS

AIGUABLAVA
Aigua Blava (€€€)
One of the gems of the Catalan coast. Many rooms are in villas in the gardens; also tennis courts and a pool.
✉ Platja de Fornells ☎ 972 62 20 58; www.aiguablava.com ⊙ Closed Nov–Feb

BEGUR
Aiguaclara (€€)
Charming hotel in an old colonial building in a central location, with stylish decor and a good restaurant.
✉ Carrer Sant Miquel 2 ☎ 972 62 29 05; www.aiguaclara.com ⊙ Closed Jan to mid-Feb

Rosa (€)
Family-run hotel in the heart of town. Bike hire available.
✉ Carrer Pi iRalló 11 ☎ 972 62 30 15; www.hotel-rosa.com ⊙ Closed Dec–Feb

BESALÚ
Comte Tallaferro (€€)
Stylish rooms in a 16th-century town house. Guests can use the swimming pool at Fonda Siqués, run by the same family.
✉ Carrer Ganganell 2 ☎ 972 591609; www.grupcalparent.com

LA BISBAL D'EMPORDÀ
Castell d'Empordà (€€€)
Luxury hotel set in a 12th-century castle, with a pool in the extensive gardens and rooms filled with art and antiques.
✉ Castell d'Empordà ☎ 972 646254; www.castelldemporda.com ⊙ Closed Jan–Feb

CALELLA DE PALAFRUGELL
Mediterrani (€€)
Long-established, welcoming hotel with sweeping views of the Mediterranean. Located near the town's restaurants.

✉ Carrer Francesc Estrabau 40 ☎ 972 61 45 00; www.hotelmediterrani.com
🕐 Closed Oct–Apr

Sant Roc (€€)

Traditional seaside hotel in a spectacular position on a rocky outcrop looking over the bay. Steps lead down to the beach.
✉ Plaça de l'Atlàntic 2 ☎ 972 61 42 50; www.santroc.com 🕐 Closed Nov–Mar

L'ESTARTIT
Santa Anna (€€)

This centrally located, family-run hotel has two swimming pools – one for children – and a good-quality restaurant (open Mar–Dec only).
✉ Carrer del Port 46–48 ☎ 972 75 13 26; www.hotelsantaanna.com

GIRONA
Bellmirall (€)

This medieval stone mansion, in the old town, has been turned into a charming hostel with simple but comfortable rooms overlooking the cathedral.
✉ Carrer Bellmirall 3 ☎ 972 20 40 09 🕐 Closed Jan–Feb

Ciutat de Girona (€€)

Cool, minimalist design hotel, close to the old town and the river.
✉ Carrer Nord 2 ☎ 972 483038; www.hotel-ciutatdegirona.com

Peninsula (€€)

Comfortable hotel in an excellent central location, beside the Pont de Pedra and close to Girona's old town quarter.
✉ Carrer Nou 3 ☎ 972 20 38 00; www.novarahotels.com

LLAFRANC
Far de Sant Sebastià (€€€)

Just nine rooms set around an interior courtyard in an old chapel high on the cliffs. Some of the rooms have magnificent sea views.
✉ Cap de Sant Sebastià ☎ 972 301639; www.elfar.net 🕐 Closed Jan

Llafranch (€€)

Stylish, comfortable hotel on the seafront promenade, with a reputation for good food. One of the first tourist hotels on the Costa Brava, and still run by the same family. Salvador Dalí was a regular visitor; the bar is lined with pictures of him with flamenco performers and the brothers who ran the hotel.

✉ Passeig de Cípsela 16 ☎ 972 30 02 08; www.hllafranch.com
🕐 Closed Nov–Dec

PALS
Mas de Torrent (€€€)

An 18th-century farmhouse, with period furniture and flower-filled gardens. Known for its innovative Catalan cuisine.

✉ Torrent, between Pals and Palafrugell ☎ 902 55 03 21; www.mastorrent.com

PERATALLADA
Cal'Aliu (€)

Simple, attractive rooms in a village house. Breakfast is included and bike rental is available.

✉ Carrer de la Roca 6 ☎ 972 63 40 61

TAMARIU
Tamariu (€€)

A small and friendly hotel right beside the beach.

✉ Passeig del Mar 2 ☎ 972 62 00 31; www.tamariu.com 🕐 Closed Dec–Feb

RESTAURANTS

BEGUR
Aiguablava (€€)

See page 58.

El Bodegón (€€€)

Fresh local fish is roasted in a wood-burning oven at this back-street restaurant in the old centre of town.

✉ Carrer Pi i Ralló 3 ☎ 972 62 20 13 🕐 Tue–Sun lunch and dinner

BESALÚ
Ca'n Quei (€)
A good-value bar on a quiet square, serving snacks, sandwiches, salads and hot meals.

✉ Plaça Sant Vicenç ☎ 972 59 00 85 ◷ Thu–Mon lunch and dinner, Tue lunch only. Closed first 2 weeks in Jul

Curia Reial (€€)
See page 59

Els Fogons de Can Llaudes (€€€)
This elegant restaurant is housed in a Romanesque chapel facing the church of Sant Pere. The emphasis is on meat and game, such as venison, wild boar and roast lamb. Booking essential.

✉ Prat de Sant Pere 6 ☎ 972 59 08 58 ◷ Wed–Mon lunch and dinner

CALELLA DE PALAFRUGELL
Can Palet (€€)
This small, attractive seafood restaurant has tables beside the beach.

✉ Carrer Calau 8 ☎ 972 61 45 45 ◷ Wed–Mon 9am–9:30pm

Tragamar (€€)
Seaside branch of a popular Barcelona restaurant chain, offering designer *tapas* and sophisticated Catalan cuisine in informal, stylish surroundings on the beachside promenade.

✉ Platja del Canadell ☎ 972 61 51 89 ◷ Daily lunch and dinner. Closed Tue in winter

Les Voltes (€€€)
See page 59.

L'ESTARTIT
Can Dalfó (€€€)
Elegant establishment near the waterfront, serving traditional Catalan dishes such as *suquet* (mixed fish platter) and *arroz con sepia* (rice with cuttlefish).

✉ Carrer Santa Anna 13, Port 10 ☎ 972 75 10 32 🕔 Wed–Mon 12:30–4, 7–11. Closed Tue and Jan

Felix (€€)

A pleasant restaurant with an informal atmosphere and a good view of the waterfront, offering a wide range of regional dishes and fresh fish.

✉ Passeig Marítim 28 ☎ 972 75 06 19 🕔 Jun–Sep daily 8:30am–2am

GIRONA

Abril (€)

Fresh, light, healthy salads, meat and fish dishes and a good-value four-course lunchtime menu are served at this pretty little bistro, with tables on the square in summer.

✉ Carrer de Santa Clara 27 ☎ 972 41 10 55 🕔 Mon–Sat 8:30–8:30

El Balcó (€€)

This Argentinian restaurant is a paradise for serious meat-lovers, with beef, veal and duck grilled to perfection over an open fire.

✉ Carrer de les Hortes 16 ☎ 972 22 31 61 🕔 Mon–Sat 1:30–4, 9–11 or midnight. Closed Sun

Le Bistrot (€)

Pancakes, salads and crusty bread pizzas at this popular old-style bistro, with tables out of doors on a pretty staircase in summer.

✉ Pujada Sant Domènec 4 ☎ 972 21 88 03 🕔 Daily 1–4, 7–midnight or later

Boira (€€)

See page 58.

Casa Marieta (€€)

This popular old standby serves traditional Catalan food, such as seafood casserole and duck with pears, in agreeably old-fashioned surroundings on an arcaded square.

✉ Plaça Independéncia 5 ☎ 972 20 10 16 🕔 Tue–Sun 1–3:30, 8–11. Closed 2 weeks in Feb

Creperie Bretonne (€€)

Delicious, authentic French pancakes and cider from Brittany served in offbeat, retro surroundings.

✉ Carrer Cort Reial 14 ☎ 972 21 81 20 🕐 Tue–Fri 1–4, 8–11 or later, Sat–Sun 1pm–midnight

Mar Plaça (€€€)

This classy fish restaurant specializes in fish soups and casseroles and also serves delicious simply grilled fresh fish.

✉ Plaça Independència 3 ☎ 972 20 59 62 🕐 Tue–Sun 1–4, 8–11

El Pou del Call (€€)

Come here for good-value Catalan cuisine with an excellent *menú del día*; located in the heart of the Jewish quarter.

✉ Carrer de la Força 14 ☎ 972 22 37 74 🕐 Mon–Sat 12:30–4, 8–11:30, Sun 12:30–4:30

La Taverna (€)

Tapas, omelettes, local sausages and cheeses, home-made patés and Basque cider all served at outdoor tables.

✉ Plaça Santa Susanna 2 ☎ 972 21 13 81 🕐 Mon–Sat 7:30am–11pm

Zanpanzar (€)

A Basque-style *tapas* bar where the *pintxos* (bite-sized open sandwiches) are laid out along the counter. You help yourself and then add up the cocktail sticks on your plate in order to settle your bill. Basque cider is a speciality.

✉ Carrer Cort Reial 12 ☎ 972 21 28 43 🕐 Mon–Fri 7am–midnight, Sat–Sun 12–4, 7–midnight

OLOT
La Deu (€€)

The famous Garrotxa potato dish *patates de la Deu* (potatoes, meat and vegetables in béchamel sauce) was invented at this traditional Catalan restaurant, which offers hearty "volcanic cooking" in a country house on the edge of town.

✉ Carretera La Deu ☎ 972 26 10 04 🕐 Mon–Sat 1–8, Sun 1–4

PALAFRUGELL
La Xicra (€€€)
Classic Empordan cooking in a village house. Speciality dishes include seafood casserole and chickpeas with baby octopus and ham.

✉ Carrer de Sant Antoni 17 ☎ 972 30 56 30 🕐 Mon, Thu–Sat 1–4, 8–11. Tue, Sun 1–4. Closed Nov

PALS
Mas de Torrent (€€€)
Innovative meat and fish dishes prepared with typical Catalan flair, in a beautiful 18th-century farmhouse.

✉ Torrent, near Pals ☎ 902 55 03 21 🕐 Daily lunch and dinner

PERATALLADA
Can Bonay (€€)
A third-generation family restaurant in a charming town house in the main square offering Catalan classics such as goose with turnips and pig's trotters with snails.

✉ Plaça de les Voltes 13 ☎ 972 63 40 34 🕐 Tue–Sun 1:30–3:30, 8:30–10:30

La Riera (€)
See page 59.

PÚBOL
Can Bosch (€)
Traditional village restaurant serving hearty portions and a good-value set lunch.

✉ Beside the castle ☎ 972 48 83 57 🕐 Daily 9–6. Closed Feb

SANT JOAN DE LES ABADESSES
Casa Rudes (€)
Casa Rudes serves home-cooked Catalan favourites such as venison and wild mushrooms in season. It has an adjoining, old-style grocery shop selling cured sausages and other local produce.

✉ Carrer Major 10 ☎ 972 72 01 15 🕐 Daily lunch, Mon–Sat dinner

SANTA PAU
Cal Sastre (€€)

Garrotxa cuisine featuring local sausages, mushrooms and beans, and located in a delightful square.

✉ Placeta dels Balls 6 ☎ 972 68 04 21 🕐 Tue–Sun lunch, Tue–Sat dinner. Closed Mon and last 3 weeks in Feb

TAMARIU
Es Dofí (€€)

This is one of the best of the many fish restaurants along the seafront.

✉ Passeig del Mar 22 ☎ 972 62 00 43 🕐 Wed–Mon 10–5. Closed Tue

SHOPPING

ARTS AND CRAFTS
Agadi
See page 64.

L'Artesanat
See page 64.

Avellí
See page 64.

Bambu Bambu

If you can't face looking at any more pottery, this large shop on La Bisbal's "ceramic street" has a huge collection of local basketware.

✉ Carrer l'Aigüeta 61, La Bisbal ☎ 972 64 23 33

La Bisbal d'Art
See page 64.

Bosch

A large pottery emporium selling everyday items like earthenware plates and cooking pots at good prices.

✉ Carrer l'Aigüeta 47, La Bisbal ☎ 972 64 38 19

La Botiga

See page 64.

El Càntir

Bright, colourful, locally made pottery sold at two shops on the main road.

✉ Carrer l'Aigüeta 45 and 126, La Bisbal ☎ 972 64 24 72

Embolic

You can watch the beautiful tapestries being woven at this workshop close to the old town walls.

✉ Avinguda Lluís Companys 22, Torroella de Montgrí ☎ 972 75 85 71

L'Estació

Ming-style vases, homages to the Catalan design gurus such as Miró and Picasso, and ceramic cartoon characters for children can all be found among the casseroles and coffee pots here.

✉ Carrer l'Aigüeta 18, La Bisbal ☎ 972 64 20 97

Fang i Art

All the pottery sold here is guaranteed made by hand in a local workshop. Look for the beautiful Arab-style water pots.

✉ Carrer l'Aigüeta 76, La Bisbal ☎ 972 64 39 43

Katy

Striking and imaginative pottery in colourful, childlike designs.

✉ Carrer l'Aigüeta 41, La Bisbal ☎ 972 64 38 44

Llensa

The big attraction of Llensa is the wide range of terracotta garden pots, including some antiques in a room at the back.

✉ Carrer l'Aigüeta 91, La Bisbal ☎ 972 64 20 71

Nadal

A retail outlet boasting a big selection of pottery for the kitchen, home and the garden.

✉ Carrer l'Aigüeta 84, La Bisbal ☎ 972 64 03 88

D'Occ Catalonia
Stylish, locally made ceramics and cosmetics are sold at this shop on the main street. There is another branch in Girona, at the entrance to the Jewish quarter at Carrer de la Força 1.
✉ Carrer l'Aigüeta 74, La Bisbal ☎ 972 641462

Pau Planes
Local potters Pau Planes and Maria Marquès produce distinctive modern designs that are on sale in two shops in the village.
✉ Plaça Major 8 and Carrer Major 9, Pals ☎ 972 63 64 02

Plats i Olles
An interesting shop with a good range of locally produced artefacts and gifts, mostly in ceramics and glass.
✉ Carrer Cavallers 33, Palafrugell ☎ 972 30 01 47

Rogenca d'Ullastret
Everything is produced in a local workshop. You can also visit the workshop and exhibition room in the centre of town at Passeig Marimon Asprer 4, on the riverside promenade.
✉ Carrer l'Aigüeta 112, La Bisbal ☎ 972 640482

Santa & Clara
See page 65.

Sclop
See page 65.

El Talleret
A range of locally produced pottery that is sold at several shops throughout the town.
✉ Carrer l'Aigüeta 37, 54 and 136, La Bisbal ☎ 972 64 27 08

Vila Clara
This is an arty pottery workshop where everything is designed and made locally. There are two shops – one at each end of the town.
✉ Carrer l'Aigüeta 56 and Carrer Sis d'Octubre 27, La Bisbal ☎ 972 64 25 79

Les Voltes

Glass and pottery. Beneath the arches in the square.

✉ Plaça de les Voltes, Peratallada ☎ 972 63 41 21

FOOD AND DRINK

Cacao Sampaka

Rich chocolatey treats, including truffles in a variety of unusual flavours.

✉ Carrer Santa Clara 45, Girona ☎ 972 20 23 41

Cal Enric

This factory shop sells a tempting selection of *galetes*, delicious local biscuits made with butter and almonds, which make a tasty souvenir to take back home.

✉ Carretera Girona 6, Castellfollit de la Roca ☎ 972 29 40 44

J Candela

This shop sells *turrón* (*torró* in Catalan), produced in the family factory, as well as a range of unusual sweets.

✉ Carrer de l'Argenteria 8, Girona ☎ 972 22 09 38

Museu de l'Embotit

The sausage museum (➤ 99) sells cured meats from the Sala factory, which has been based here for more than 150 years.

✉ Carretera Girona 10, Castellfollit de la Roca ☎ 972 29 44 63

El Rebost del Comtat

A museum of local history and crafts with a cheese and sausage shop attached, where you can taste before you buy.

✉ Plaça Llibertat 14, Besalú ☎ 972 59 03 07

MARKETS

Mercat Municipal

This indoor market near the Plaça de Catalunya in Girona has stalls selling a wide range of meat, fish and cheeses, fresh fruit and vegetables, as well as ready-prepared meals. It's a good place to stock up on provisions for a picnic. On Saturdays there are also outdoor produce markets in the square which are lively and colourful.

✉ Plaça Salvador Espriu, Girona ⏱ Mon–Sat 7–1:30

Mercat Semanal

Girona's weekly markets take place on Tuesday and Saturday, on the edge of Parc de la Devesa. On Saturdays a flower market is set up on the Rambla, along with arts and crafts stalls on Pont de Pedra.

✉ Passeig de la Devesa, Girona ⏱ Tue, Sat all year

ENTERTAINMENT

BARS AND CLUBS

Sala de Ball

Dance hall and nightclub where the locals dance the tango to live orchestras at weekends.

✉ Passeig de la Devesa 21, Girona ☎ 972 20 14 39

Sunset Jazz Club

Smoky jazz bar with live modern jazz Saturday and Sunday nights.

✉ Carrer Jaume Pons i Martí 12, Girona ☎ 872 08 01 45

MUSIC FESTIVALS

Calella de Palafrugell

See page 76.

Girona

See page 76.

Olot

See page 76–77.

Palafrugell

See page 77.

Torroella de Montgrí

See page 77.

Figueres and the North Coast

This region stretches from the wide Gulf of Roses, with its marshes, estuaries and endless beach, to the wild northern coastline, where the Pyrenees drop into the sea. Foreigners have long been drawn to these shores – it was here that the Greeks and Romans established their first ports – and the area around trendy Cadaqués has become the most fashionable stretch of the Costa Brava.

Figueres

The north coast is inextricably linked with Salvador Dalí, whose surreal landscapes owe much to the scenery around Cap de Creus. Take the twisting coast road from Portbou to El Port de la Selva, with the mountains on one side and the sea on the other, then drive across the headland, with its wind-sculpted rocks, and you soon see how the artist and the landscape were made for each other.

FIGUERES

The capital of the Alt Empordà region would be just another county town, were it not for the influence of its most famous son, Salvador Dalí. Tourists pour in by the bus-load to see his surreal theatre-museum (➤ 52–53) and Figueres is enjoying a new-found prosperity as a result. For centuries it was an unassuming market town, created by royal charter in 1267; now it is firmly established on the Spanish tourist circuit.

Long before Dalí's birth in 1904, Figueres had a reputation for creativity and new ideas – federalism, Republicanism, Modernist art. The Utopian socialist Narcís Monturiol, claimed as the inventor of the submarine, was born in the same street as Dalí; it was another local resident, Pep Ventura, who created the modern form of the *sardana* in the mid-19th century.

➕ 8C

ℹ Plaça del Sol, tel: 972 50 31 55

Barri Antic

Between the Rambla and the Dalí museum lies the centre of old Figueres, now a network of pedestrian shopping streets. Several of these streets converge on Plaça Ajuntament, a peaceful, arcaded square that was once the gateway to the city. The street names leading from the square show Figueres' historical importance as the crossroads of northern Catalonia – Carrer Girona to the south, Carrer Besalú to the west, Carrer La Jonquera to the north and Carrer Peralada to the east.

 Lizarran (€, ➤ 154)

Castell de Sant Ferran

This star-shaped citadel, begun in 1753 as a defence against the French, was once claimed to be the second-largest fortress in Europe. During the Napoleonic Wars it was captured by French forces, who imprisoned and later executed the hero of the Girona resistance, Alvarez de Castro. From 1904 to 1933 it was a high-security prison, holding some of Spain's most dangerous criminals.

On a one-hour, self-guided audio-tour you can stroll around the castle ramparts and visit the parade ground, chapel and vaulted stables. Even when it is closed you can get a feel for its vast size by walking around the 3km (2-mile) path that encircles the castle walls.

✉ Pujada del Castell ☎ 972 50 79 16 🕓 1 Jul–15 Sep daily 10:30–8; 16 Sep–Jun daily 10:30–3 💲 Inexpensive ❓ Jeep tours of ramparts, dinghy trips of underground cisterns at weekends and summer; reservations essential

Monestir de Vilabertran

In the village of Vilabertran, 2km (1.2 miles) from Figueres, is an Augustinian abbey that is considered to be one of the finest examples of Catalan Romanesque architecture. The 11th-century basilica, with three aisles, three apses and a tall, square belltower, still stands, together with a 12th-century cloister with plant motifs carved on its capitals. In summer the abbey is the setting for classical music concerts. Among the other buildings are the original chapter house and wine cellar, and a 15th-century Gothic abbots' palace.

✉ On the road from Figueres to Peralada ☎ 972 50 87 87 ⏲ Jun–Sep Tue–Sun 10–1, 3–6; Oct–May Tue–Sun 10–1, 3–5 ❓ Classical music festival, Aug–Sep

Museu de l'Empordà

The museum of local art and history was established in 1876 and moved to its present site on the Rambla in 1971. It contains archaeological discoveries from the Iberian, Greek and Roman periods, and a collection of 19th- and 20th-century Catalan art. There are several paintings by Antoni Tàpies, one by Dalí and a lithograph donated by Joan Miró. Artists from Figueres are well represented in the section on Empordan realism. There is also a gallery dedicated to the painters of the Olot School.

✉ Rambla 2 ☎ 972 50 23 05 ⏲ Tue–Sat 11–7, Sun 11–2 ✋ Inexpensive (free with entrance ticket for Dalí museum)

Museu del Joguet de Catalunya

In the old Hotel Paris, this toy museum started from one man's collection. Over 3,000 traditional toys are displayed, from cardboard horses to nativity scenes, including a teddy bear that once belonged to Salvador Dalí's sister.

✉ Carrer Sant Pere 1 ☎ 972 50 45 85 ⏲ Jun–Sep Mon–Sat 10–7, Sun 11–6; Jan–May, Oct–Dec Tue–Sat 10–8, Sun 11–6 ✋ Moderate

Rambla

The heart of Figueres is its Rambla, an attractive tree-lined boulevard built over an old stream with small squares at either end. Whenever he was far from home, Dalí used to reminisce about Figueres' Thursday market, and the pavement cafes on the Rambla on market day are still the best place to get a feel for the pulse of the town. There are two good museums here (► opposite), and several Modernist houses, designed by local artist, Josep Azemar.

Nearby, in Plaça Josep Pla, is the Cine-Teatre Jardí, a spectacular *Modernista* theatre, which was built in 1914.

🍴 Café Hotel Paris (€, ► 154)

Teatre-Museu Dalí

Best places to see, ► 52–53.

a walk around Figueres

Start at the station. Cross the small park of Plaça Estació and fork right along Carrer Pompeu Fabra.

Turn right at the end of this street to reach the old grain market, Plaça del Gra, where a market is still held three times a week. Cross this square and take Carrer Concepció to reach Plaça de la Palmera. Turn left towards the Rambla.

A monument to Narcís Monturiol (➤ 130) dominates the eastern end of the Rambla. Walk down the central avenue, then take Carrer Lasauca, ahead on the left, passing the Hotel Durán, an old haunt of Salvador Dalí. Cross the ring road at the end of this street to reach the tourist office in Plaça del Sol.

From the tourist office turn left along Avinguda Salvador Dalí and left again to reach Parc Bosc, a shady and peaceful retreat from the crowds. After exploring the park, return to Avinguda Salvador Dalí, then cross the road to Carrer Pep Ventura straight ahead.

Emerging on Pujada del Castell, look left for your first glimpse of the Dalí museum (➤ 52–53). Cross this street into Carrer Besalú. To visit the museum, one of the most visited in Spain, turn left along Carrer Sant Pere; otherwise, continue straight ahead into the town hall square, Plaça Ajuntament.

Cross this square and take Carrer Peralada to reach the large, ochre-coloured Modernist building, Casino Menestral. Turn right on to Carrer Ample. At the end of the street, look for the plaque opposite, denoting the house on Carrer Monturiol where Salvador Dalí was born. Turn left to return to Plaça de la Palmera and retrace your steps to the station.

Distance 2km (1.2 miles)
Time 1 hour
Start/end point Figueres station ✚ 8C 🚌 To Figueres bus station on Plaça Estació 🚃 Trains from Girona and Portbou
Lunch Durán (€€, ➤ 59)

The North Coast

CADAQUÉS
Best places to see, ➤ 38–39.

CAP DE CREUS
This jagged peninsula, where the Pyrenees jut into the sea, is a place of savage beauty and vicious winds. Salvador Dalí lived just down the road at Portlligat (➤ 142–143), and as you stand on the headland gazing down into secluded creeks it is impossible not to see Dalíesque images in the rocks, carved by nature into ever more surreal shapes. This is where the *tramuntana*, the legendary north wind that strikes fear into sailors and fishermen, is at its most violent. If you come when the wind is blowing you will struggle to stay on your feet.

The easiest way to reach the cape is from Cadaqués (➤ 38–39), on a narrow road that snakes across the headland. There is also a coastal footpath from Portlligat, difficult to follow but with the reward of seeing this craggy landscape at its isolated best and dipping into hidden coves along the way. The road ends at a lighthouse, where you can walk on to the slate cliffs and look down over the seascape of deep turquoise water, small islands and rocky coves. This is the easternmost point in mainland Spain and if you come here at dawn you can watch the sun rise over the Iberian peninsula. Seabirds migrate here in winter and wheatears and rock thrushes build their nests in spring, when the cliffs are carpeted with wild flowers and the headland is scented with rosemary and lavender. Swifts and pipits arrive in summer.

✚ 12B 🍴 Cap de Creus (€–€€, ➤ 58) 🚌 Cadaqués, 8km (5 miles) away

❓ *Sardana* dancing at sunrise on 1 Jan

ℹ Palau de l'Abat, Monestir de Sant Pere de Rodes

Parc Natural de Cap de Creus
☎ 972 19 31 91 🕐 Daily 10–2, 3–6 ❓ Walking and cycling trails from Sant Pere de Rodes

CASTELLO D'EMPÚRIES

Castelló d'Empúries was the seat of the Counts of Empúries
during the Middle Ages and many of its buildings date from then.
Its greatest glory is the basilica of Santa Maria, an early Gothic
church built on the site of a Romanesque cathedral and considered
the second church of Girona province, after Girona Cathedral itself.
It is worth visiting just to see the magnificently sculpted portal;
inside there is a Romanesque double font and a fine alabaster
altarpiece by Vicenç Borràs. Other buildings of note are a 14th-

century prison and the El Rentador wash house, with a porticoed atrium, fountain and view of the basilica through its arches.

The nearby resort of Empúriabrava was built in 1967 on the Muga river delta. It consists of a large marina and an extensive network (30km/18.5 miles) of canals, plus hundreds of near-identical whitewashed holiday villas, each with their own private mooring. There is a long beach and facilities for watersports, as well as boat trips on the canals and around the coast. There's also a small aerodrome offering parachuting and pleasure flights. The resort is well laid-out and attractive, but lacks any authentic Catalan feel.

The decision to build Empúriabrava on former marshland led indirectly to the creation of the Aiguamolls de l'Empordà nature reserve (➤ 48–49).

✚ 9C 🍽 Portal de la Gallarda (€€), Carrer Pere Estany 🚌 From Cadaqués, Figueres and Girona ❓ Market on Tue; La Verge de Candelera, 2 Feb; Diada del Carme festival at Empúriabrava, 16 Jul; Festa de Sant Llorenç, 10 Aug; Terra dels Trobadors (minstrel festival), 11 Sep.

ℹ Plaça Jaume I, tel: 972 15 62 33

COLERA

This small resort close to the French border has two large pebble beaches set into a horseshoe bay, with a fishing harbour at one end. A flight of steps from the northern beach leads to the Art Parc, where you can clamber over a collection of brightly coloured tile sculptures. Near here is the tiny train station. A road from the station leads to the next bay at Cala Rovellada, with its own small beach.

✚ 10B 🍽 Garbet (€€), Carretera de Llança Sur, Km 3 🚌 From Figueres, Girona and Portbou

EMPÚRIES

Best places to see, ➤ 42–43.

L'ESCALA

What was once just a fishing port has grown into a major holiday resort. There are several good beaches to either side of the town, especially at Cala Montgó to the south. Anchovies have been salted here ever since the Greeks landed at nearby Empúries (➤ 42–43); local sardines are another good buy at the fish auctions, which take place by the harbour weekday afternoons.

🚌 10E 🍴 L'Esculapy (€€, ➤ 153) 🚌 Buses from Figueres, Girona, Palafrugell and Torroella de Montgrí ❓ Market on Sun
ℹ️ Plaça de les Escolas 1, tel: 972 77 06 03

LLANÇÀ

Llançà was built 2km (1.2 miles) back from its harbour in an effort to deter pirates. Life in the old town centres around the Plaça Major. The busy harbour, with beaches to either side, has a pleasant promenade lined with fish restaurants. Climb the rocky outcrop on the edge of the marina for great views of Cap de Creus (➤ 136) poking out to sea.
www.llanca.cat

✚ 10B 🍴 La Brasa (€€, ➤ 154) 🚌 From Figueres and El Port de la Selva 🚆 Trains from Figueres, Girona and Portbou ❓ Market on Wed
ℹ Camprodón 16–18, tel: 972 38 08 55

MONESTIR DE SANT PERE DE RODES

Best places to see, ➤ 46–47.

PARC NATURAL DE L'AIGUAMOLLS DE L'EMPORDÀ

Best places to see, ➤ 48–49.

PERALADA

The moated Renaissance castle that dominates this village is better known these days as Catalonia's most stylish casino (➤ 156). Entrance to the **castle museum,** with its collections of glass and ceramics and the largest private library in Spain, also gives access to the 14th-century Carmelite convent within the castle walls. Some tours also include a tasting of *cava* from the castle cellars. Peralada lies at the centre of the Empordà–Costa Brava wine demarcation and the owners of the castle, the Mateu family, produce some excellent wines.

✚ 8C ❓ International music festival in the castle grounds, Jul–Aug
ℹ Plaça Peixateria 6, tel: 972 53 88 40

Museu del Castell

☎ 972 53 81 25 🕐 Guided tours daily from 10am (closed Mon 16 Sep–Jun)
✋ Moderate

EL PORT DE LA SELVA

With its whitewashed houses facing an attractive harbour, this small resort on the edge of the Cap de Creus peninsula looks every bit the timeless Mediterranean fishing village that it almost is. Fishing boats still set out each day to gather the anchovies for which El Port de la Selva is known, but fishing is slowly giving way to tourism. The water is shallow, the beach is long and sandy, and there is good windsurfing in the sheltered bay. The Serra de Rodes mountains, with the monastery of Sant Pere de Rodes (➤ 46–47) looking down, provide the perfect backdrop.

🔡 10B 🍴 Ca l'Herminda (€€), Carrer Illa 7 🚌 From Cadaqués, Figueres and Llançà 🚢 Excursions to Cap de Creus 🛈 Market on Fri

🛈 Carrer del Mar 1, tel: 972 38 70 73

PORTLLIGAT

This small fishing village on the outskirts of Cadaqués (➤ 38–39), with boats moored on the beach and the gentle waters of the bay enclosed by an offshore island, is where the painter Salvador Dalí made his home. He first moved here with his future wife Gala in 1930 and stayed permanently from 1948 until her death in 1982. His house, **Casa-Museu Salvador Dalí,** built over the ruins of a pair of fishermen's cottages, contains typical Dalíesque touches – eggs on the roof, camels in the garden and a swimming pool modelled on the Alhambra in Granada. It is now open to the public, largely as Dalí left it, and a visit here gives a fascinating insight into the artist's troubled mind. Only a few visitors are allowed in at a time, so booking is essential. In summer it is also possible to take a trip on Dalí's old fishing boat, *Gala*, to Cap de Creus (➤ 136).

✚ 11C 🍴 Chez Pierre (€€) 🚌 Cadaqués

Casa-Museu Salvador Dalí

www.salvador-dali.org

☎ 972 25 10 15 🕐 15 Jun–15 Sep daily 9:30–9; 15 Mar–14 Jun, 16 Sep–6 Jan Tue–Sun 10:30–6 ✋ Expensive ❓ Advance booking is essential. Boat trips daily 10–8 in summer ☎ 617 46 57 57

a drive from Portlligat

This drive takes in all the major sights associated with the life of Salvador Dalí, beginning at his home in Portlligat and ending at his final resting-place in Figueres. It also recreates the macabre journey made by Dalí's chauffeur, Artur Caminada, on 10 June, 1982, with the body of Dalí's wife, Gala, in the back seat. She had stipulated that she wanted to die in her castle at Púbol and when she died at Portlligat instead it was Caminada's job to carry her "home".

Begin by the beach in Portlligat (▶ 142–143) and follow signs to Cadaqués (▶ 38–39). Just before reaching Cadaqués, turn right towards Roses (▶ 50–51).

Continue on this road as it winds across the cape, bypassing Roses to head towards Figueres.

> *When you see Castelló d'Empúries on your right, turn left at the roundabout towards Sant Pere Pescador (► 146–147).*

You now cross the Empordan plain, passing through a succession of small villages. Turn right in Sant Pere Pescador to reach Torroella de Fluvià, then turn left on to the C31. Follow this long straight road, signposted to La Bisbal, through Verges and Ultramort to Parlavà.

> *Turn right at the traffic lights in Parlavà. Reaching the Girona road, turn right again and take the next left to visit the Castell Gala Dalí, Púbol (► 40–41). After visiting the castle, return to the Girona road. Before reaching Girona, turn right on to the N11 towards Figueres.*

This road runs parallel to the motorway towards France with occasional glimpses of the Pyrenees to your left. After 30 minutes, take the exit for Figueres. The Dalí museum (► 52–53) is in the centre of town.

Distance 115km (71 miles)
Time 2.5 hours plus lunch and visit to Castell Gala Dalí, Púbol
Start point Portlligat ➕ 11C
End point Figueres ➕ 8C
Lunch Can Bosch (€), Púbol, tel: 972 48 83 57

PORTBOU

"Benvinguts" ("Welcome"), says a sign in Catalan at the entrance to this town, leaving day-trippers from France in no doubt that they have arrived in Catalonia, as well as Spain. The opening of the international railway station in 1878 transformed this fishing village into a busy transport hub and there is now a road across the border as well, to the French port of Cerbère. High-speed trains from Paris to Barcelona will eventually pass through Portbou. At the centre of town, the Rambla de Catalunya is an attractive tree-lined boulevard and there is another pretty promenade in front of the pebble beach.

🚲 10A 🍴 L'Ancora (€€), Passeig de la Sardana 3
🚆 Trains from Figueres and Girona
ℹ️ Passeig Lluis Companys, tel: 972 12 51 61

ROSES

Best places to see,
➤ 50–51.

SANT PERE PESCADOR

The village of "St Peter the Fisherman" was built 3km (2 miles) back from the sea to provide a safe haven from pirates, with the unforeseen result that it has largely escaped the Costa Brava's tourist boom. While other fishing ports have been transformed into mass-market, modern resorts, Sant Pere Pescador remains a peaceful, workaday place, where farmers and fruit-growers mingle with occasional foreign tourists on the banks of the River Fluvià.

There is a 17th-century baroque church and the remains of an old castle, but the real attraction of Sant Pere Pescador is its beach, a long and lonely stretch of sand on the shores of the Gulf of Roses. There are no high-rise hotels here, just campsites among the dunes; come out of season when the campsites are closed and you can have sweeping views of the bay all to yourself.

The coastline is protected from development by being part of the Aiguamolls de l'Empordà natural park (➤ 48–49). The protected area also includes the banks of the Fluvià, on both sides of the village. You can walk along well-marked paths to reach the Illa de Caramany, a wooded island and bird reserve created when the course of the river was diverted in 1979.

Close to Sant Pere Pescador are a number of interesting medieval villages, rising above the flat Empordan plain. Sant Miquel de Fluvià is best known for its 11th-century Romanesque abbey, while Sant Tomàs de Fluvià also has an 11th-century priory church, with recently discovered murals.

✚ 9D 🍴 Can Trona (€€), Plaça Major 9 🚌 From L'Escala, Figueres and Palafrugell

SERRA DE L'ALBERA

The Albera mountain range, on the French border, is where the Pyrenees begin their long descent into the sea. It is a place of frontier villages and mountain passes, of vineyards, olive groves and cork forests and, in the north, a natural park that offers excellent walking along tracks once used by smugglers and refugees.

The park's information centre is at Espolla, a village of narrow streets huddled around a church. Espolla is at the heart of the Costa Brava's wine industry, and at cooperatives outside the village you can taste and buy the local *Vi de l'Empordà*. The area around Espolla is also known to archaeologists as the place with the greatest concentration of megalithic monuments in Catalonia, with tombs, rock carvings and standing stones dating back to 3500BC. One of the easiest to reach is the Dolmen de la Cabana Arqueta, a burial chamber between Espolla and the next village of Sant Climent de Sescebes. Other paths from Espolla lead to the Dolmen del Barranc, with human and animal figures carved into the roof, and to the standing stones at Rabós d'Empordà, from where a mountain track leads to the 11th-century monastery of Sant Quirze de Colera.

A hair-raising drive from Sant Climent, best attempted in an off-road vehicle, snakes across the mountains to the Castell de Requesens, a restored medieval castle on the site of an earlier fortress. A good road from here, through the village of Cantallops, leads to the border crossing at La Jonquera, where lorries thunder past on the motorway from Paris to Barcelona.

✚ 8A 🍴 Restaurants in Espolla, Garriguella and Sant Climent (€–€€)

🚌 Bus from Figueres to Espolla

Parc Natural de Serra de l'Albera

ℹ Carrer del Mossèn Amadeu Sudrià 3, Espolla, tel: 972 54 50 79

HOTELS

CADAQUÉS

Llané Petit (€€)

Beachside hotel on the southern side of the bay, close to the town centre. On the way into town you pass Port Alguer, a scene from a 1924 Dalí painting that has hardly changed since he captured it.

✉ Carrer Dr Bartomeus 37 ☎ 972 25 10 20; www.llanepetit.com

🕓 Closed 8 Jan–22 Mar

Playa Sol (€€)

Seaside hotel with a swimming pool in the gardens, tennis court and a small beach decked out with fishing boats directly opposite.

✉ Platja Pianc 3 ☎ 972 25 81 00; www.playasol.com 🕓 Closed Nov–Feb

Rocamar (€€)

Traditional seaside hotel with a seawater pool and steps down to a rocky cove.

✉ Carrer Verge del Carme s/n ☎ 972 25 81 50; www.rocamar.com

CASTELLÓ D'EMPÚRIES

Canet (€€)

Town-centre hotel with a swimming pool in its interior courtyard.

✉ Plaça Joc de la Pilota 2 ☎ 972 25 03 40; www.hotelcanet.com 🕓 Closed Nov–Feb

Hotel de la Moneda (€€)

Four-star hotel in a restored 17th-century mansion in the old Jewish quarter. Facilities here include a pool and free internet access.

✉ Plaça de la Moneda 8 ☎ 972 15 86 02; www.hoteldelamoneda.com

🕓 Closed 11 Dec–8 Mar

EMPÚRIES

Hostal Empuriés (€€)

Newly refurbished, old-style beach hotel, near the Greek and Roman ruins.

✉ Platja de Portitxol ☎ 972 77 02 07; www.hostalempuries.com

FIGUERES
Durán (€€)
An atmospheric, old-world hotel in the centre of town, where Salvador Dalí used to meet his friends for lunch. It also has one of the finest restaurants in Figueres.

✉ Carrer Lasauca 5 ☎ 972 50 12 50; www.hotelduran.com

Empordà (€€)
This stylish hotel was the birthplace of the new Catalan cuisine and is still an essential place of pilgrimage for food-lovers.

✉ Avinguda Salvador Dalí 170 ☎ 972 50 05 62; www.hotelemporda.com

Rambla (€€)
An attractive, family-run hotel with comfortable rooms, exuding a warm and welcoming atmosphere. Breakfast is served with a personal touch.

✉ Rambla 33 ☎ 972 67 60 20; www.hotelrambla.net

LLANÇÀ
Grifeu (€€)
Grifeu's excellent seafront location gives direct access to the beach, and the front rooms offer sweeping sea views. The restaurant has a large pleasant terrace for outdoor dining.

✉ Carretera de Portbou 36 ☎ 972 38 00 50 ⏰ Closed Nov–Holy Week

PERALADA
Golf Peralada (€€€)
Five-star golf and spa resort located at the centre of the golf course. Among the facilities is a vinotherapy wine spa.

✉ Carrer Rocabertí ☎ 972 538830; www.golfperalada.com

EL PORT DE LA SELVA
Porto Cristo (€€)
A comfortable three-star hotel, set just back from the beach in a restored 19th-century house.

✉ Carrer Major 69 ☎ 972 38 70 62; www.hotelportocristo.com ⏰ Closed Dec–Jan

PORTLLIGAT

Calina (€€)

This apartment-style hotel, close to the beach, has a series of self-catering apartments set around a swimming pool.

✉ Portlligat ☎ 972 25 88 51; www.hotelcalina.com ⏰ Closed Nov–Feb

Portlligat (€€)

A peaceful, two-star hotel with a swimming pool and views over Dalí's house and out to sea.

✉ Portlligat ☎ 972 25 81 62 ⏰ Closed 3 Nov–4 Dec

ROSES

Almadraba Park (€€€)

Four-star hotel with modern facilities, on a rocky cliff overlooking the cove of Almadrava.

✉ Platja de Almadrava ☎ 972 25 65 50; www.almadrabapark.com
⏰ Closed Nov–Mar

Vistabella (€€€)

This five-star hotel, beside the beach at Canyelles, has its own landing-stage for boats and offers spa-like treatments, ranging from massage to Turkish baths.

✉ Avinguda Díaz Pacheco 26 ☎ 972 25 62 00; www.vistabellahotel.com
⏰ Closed mid-Oct to mid-Mar

RESTAURANTS

CADAQUÉS

Can Rafa (€€€)

Top-quality restaurant with a good selection of fish and shellfish dishes, plus a great wine list. The dining room is adorned with photographs of Cadaqués in bygone times, and there's outdoor eating on the terrace.

✉ Passeig Marítim 7 ☎ 972 15 94 01 ⏰ Tue–Mon 12–3:30, 7:30–11; Jul–Aug daily

Cuatro (€€)

See page 58.

La Sirena (€€)
Fresh fish and vegetarian choices in this intimate restaurant, hidden away in the back streets of the Jewish quarter.

✉ Carrer d'es Call ☎ 972 25 89 74 ◷ Wed–Sun lunch and dinner

CAP DE CREUS
Cap de Creus (€–€€)
See page 58.

EMPÚRIES
Mesón del Conde (€€)
The best of the restaurants in the village of Sant Martí d'Empúries is just a short walk from the ruins. In spring try grilled *calçots*, a local onion served with *romesco* sauce.

✉ Plaça Major, Sant Martí d'Empúries ☎ 972 77 03 06 ◷ Tue–Sat 9–6, Sun 9am–midnight

L'ESCALA
L'Esculapy (€€)
L'Esculapy is renowned for its oven-baked pizzas, barbecued vegetables and carpaccios. It has an attractive garden terrace facing the Romanesque church for outdoor dining, with magnificent views of the Bay of Roses.

✉ Plaça Major 1, Sant Marti d'Empúries ☎ 972 77 00 53 ◷ Daily 1–3:30, 7–10:30. Closed Jan

Els Pescadors (€€€)
Traditional Catalan cooking using top-quality local ingredients – grilled fish, fresh seafood and *sarsuela* fish casserole.

✉ Carrer Port d'en Perris 3 ☎ 972 77 07 28 ◷ Fri–Wed 12:30–4, 7:30–11. Closed Nov

FIGUERES
Antaviana (€€)
Stylish Catalan and French cuisine with an emphasis on duck – try the *carpaccio* of duck breast or the beef in Cabrales (blue cheese) sauce.

✉ Carrer Llers 5 ☎ 972 51 03 77 🕔 Wed–Sun 1–3:30, 8:30–11. Closed mid-Feb to 1 Mar

Café Hotel Paris (€)

There's a good choice of reasonably priced dishes and *tapas* at this informal restaurant. The terrace out on the Rambla is ideal for outdoor dining.

✉ Rambla 10 ☎ 972 50 07 13 🕔 Daily 9am–11pm

Durán (€€)

See page 59.

Empordà (€€€)

This famous hotel, just outside Figueres on the old road to France, has a magnificent garden terrace, where traditional Empordan cooking is served up with modern flair. The former chef here, Josep Mercader, is considered to be the founder of Modern Catalan cuisine.

✉ Antiga Carretera de França ☎ 972 50 05 62 🕔 Daily lunch and dinner

Lizarran (€)

The long bar is laden with a good selection of tasty *tapas*. There's a lively atmosphere and it's usually buzzing with locals.

✉ Carrer Monturiol 3 ☎ 972 50 66 67 🕔 Daily 9am–11:30pm

Mesón Asador (€€€)

This stylish and elegant restaurant serves a good selection of top-notch meat and fish dishes.

✉ Pujada del Castell 4 ☎ 972 51 01 04 🕔 Mon–Sat 12:30–4, 8–11. Closed Jun

LLANÇÀ
La Brasa (€€)

Local squid and anchovies, seafood casserole and charcoal-grilled meat, served on a pretty terrace just back from the harbour.

✉ Plaça Catalunya 6 ☎ 972 38 02 02 🕔 Jul–Aug daily lunch and dinner. Closed Mon eve and Tue Sep–Jun

PERALADA
Mas Moli (€€€)
Roast lamb and suckling pig, cooked in an old-style wood oven, in the setting of an old mill.

✉ Carretera Antiga de Vilabertran ☎ 972 53 82 81 🕒 Tue–Sat 1–3:30, 8–10:15, Sun 1–3:30. Closed Jan

ROSES
El Bulli (€€€)
Quite simply one of the finest restaurants in Spain. Book ahead.

✉ Cala Montjoi ☎ 972 15 04 57 🕒 Apr–Jun Wed–Sun dinner only; Jul–Sep daily

Flor de Lis (€€€)
Sophisticated French and seafood cuisine in a pretty cottage in the back streets.

✉ Carrer Coscanilles 47 ☎ 972 25 43 16 🕒 Wed–Mon dinner only. Closed Nov–Easter

La Llar (€€€)
Creative Catalan cuisine in a delightfully restored farmhouse just outside the town. The adventurous can try the "surprise menu".

✉ Carretera Figueres Km 4 ☎ 972 25 53 68 🕒 Fri–Tue 1–3:15, 8–10, Wed–Thu 1–3:15. Closed first 2 weeks in Feb, last 2 weeks in Nov

SHOPPING

FASHION AND GIFTS
Disennium
See page 64.

Estevez
See page 65.

MARKETS
Cadaqués – Mon; Castelló d'Empúries – Tue; L'Escala – Sun; Figueres – Tue, Thu, Sat; Llançà – Wed; El Port de la Selva – Fri; Roses – Sun

WINE
La Botiga del Celler
Wines from the castle cellars, including some fine cavas and sparkling wines.

✉ Plaça del Carme 1, Peralada ☎ 972 53 80 11

ENTERTAINMENT

CASINO
Casino Castell de Peralada
Tapestries line the walls of this moated Renaissance castle where you can play roulette, blackjack or *boule* in an atmosphere of elegance, luxury and fine dining.

✉ Carrer Sant Joan s/n ☎ 972 53 81 25 ⏰ Daily 7pm–4am

CLUB
L'Hostal
Considered to be one of the foremost clubs along the coast, L'Hostal is adorned with photos of Salvador Dalí, who was a frequent visitor and who once spent an evening there with Mick Jagger and Gabriel García Marquéz. The club offers Dixieland-style jazz and rock music until the early hours.

✉ Passeig del Mar 8, Cadaqués ☎ 972 25 80 00 ⏰ Daily 5pm–5am

MUSIC FESTIVALS
Cadaqués
See page 76.

Castelló d'Empúries
See page 76.

Figueres
A music festival takes place each August and September in the old monastery and church of Vilabertran.

☎ 972 50 01 17

Peralada
See page 77.

The South

Anyone who visited the Costa Brava in 1950 would not recognize this region today. Huge concrete resorts have been created out of little more than fishing harbours, and in summer the coastline reverberates to the sound of the disco beat. Resorts like Lloret de Mar and Platja d'Aro led the way into mass tourism and they are still among the busiest in Spain.

□ Vic

□ Mataró

Not everywhere on the south coast has been changed by tourism. Sant Feliu de Guíxols and Tossa de Mar are popular resorts, but their old towns retain a lot of charm. Blanes and Palamós are still fishing ports as well as tourist centres. Even on the most crowded stretch of coastline it is still possible to find a hidden cove, a reminder of what the Costa Brava used to be before the tourists took over.

BLANES

The Costa Brava starts at Sa Palomera, a rocky promontory halfway along the beach, and continues north all the way to France. Once used for shelter by the town's fishing fleet, the promontory has the remains of an old fire-tower – a primitive lighthouse – at its summit and it is still lit up by fire each year during the Costa Brava's international fireworks contest in July.

Climb on to Sa Palomera, passing the fishing boats that are washed up on the shingle beach, for some of the best views of Blanes. South of here, the beach stretches on, as far as the eye can see, passing hotels, campsites and the mouth of the River Tordera at the start of the Costa Maresme (► 161). To the north, a wide promenade with gardens, play areas and restaurant tables on the street leads around to the town's attractive, and still busy, fishing harbour.

Blanes is still a working fishing port, where the arrival of the fleet each evening is followed by an animated auction in the fish market – you can watch it all happening from the upstairs bar. Fishermen mend their nets, old men sit on the sea walls and the sailors' chapel of Nostra Senyora de l'Esperança is adorned with nautical themes. Blanes may be one of the Costa Brava's largest resorts, but with a population of more than 40,000 it has managed to absorb the tourists without losing its soul.

The old town, just behind the seafront, has survived almost unscathed, with Gothic churches, medieval houses, fountains, shrines and a lively daily produce market. Out of season this is a real Catalan town, best experienced during the sunset promenade when everyone from grandmothers to tiny children put on their best clothes and stroll beside the sea.

Just above the town is the **Mar i Murtra** botanic garden, dramatically situated on a clifftop. There is a splendid collection of South American cactus plants, plus Californian and Chilean palms, spiny aloe from South Africa and a charming Mediterranean garden with olive, pine and tamarisk trees dropping down towards the sea. From the Linnaeus rotunda you can look down over a small cove of sparkling turquoise water and cliffs where the bushes grow wild out of the rocks. This is a very special and peaceful place, even for those who have little interest in plants. You can walk around the guided trail in less than an hour, but you could easily spend a day here, with a good book and a picnic, enjoying the sun and the shade and the sound of the sea.

The road beyond the gardens continues to the small beach and former tuna-fishing port at Cala Sant Francesc, where there is a beach bar in summer. You can also walk or drive from the gardens to the Castell de Sant Joan, an 11th-century castle and 15th-century hermitage with sweeping views of the town's beach.

🚇 19M 🍴 El Port (€–€€€, ➤ 59) 🚌 From Girona and Lloret de Mar
🚆 From Figueres and Girona 🚢 To other south coast resorts in summer
ℹ️ Passeig de Catalunya 2, tel: 972 33 03 48

Mar i Murtra

✉️ Passeig Karl Faust 9 ☎ 972 33 08 26 🕐 Jun–Sep daily 9–8; Apr–May, Oct daily 9–6; Nov–Mar daily 10–5 ✋ Moderate 🚌 From Plaça de Catalunya

CALDES DE MALAVELLA

This market town, 15km (9 miles) south of Girona, has been famous for its hot springs since Roman times: recent excavations uncovered the remains of two Roman spas. The town enjoyed a revival during the mid-19th century when it took advantage of the European fashion for "taking the waters". Dr Modest Furest marketed its bottled water under the name Vichy Catalan – a name seen on mineral water bottles throughout Spain to this day. People still come to Caldes to take the waters at the two spa hotels, built around the turn of the 20th century in neoclassical and Modernist style. They offer a range of health and beauty treatments and are particularly recommended for those with digestive and respiratory disorders.

Caldes is at the centre of the wooded Selva landscape and would make a good base for a healthy walking, cycling or horse-riding holiday.

🚩 19J 🍴 Delicius (€€), Avinguda del Dr Furest 32 🚌 Buses from Girona and Palafrugell 🚆 Trains from Figueres and Girona ❓ Market on Tue

CALONGE

The old village of Calonge is split into two parts: the medieval centre, 2km (1.2 miles) from the sea, dominated by its Gothic castle; and the modern tourist resort of Sant Antoni de Calonge, with hotels, villas and campsites strung out along the coast road between Palamós and Platja d'Aro. From the village there are some pleasant drives through forests of cork and holm oak – north to La Bisbal (► 95), or west to Romanyà de la Selva, where a 4,000-year-old burial chamber stands in a lonely spot in the woods, surrounded by a stone circle.

✚ 22J 🍴 Restaurants and bars in Sant Antoni de Calonge (€–€€) 🚌 Buses from Girona, Palafrugell and Palamós ❓ Markets: Calonge, Thu; Sant Antoni de Calonge, Wed

COSTA MARESME

This stretch of "marshy coast", which runs south from Blanes, is very different in character from the Costa Brava. Nobody would call it rugged – this is a narrow, flat coastal strip, where the beaches are mostly artificial and the villages are cut off from the sea by a busy highway and railway line. The resorts here are mainly used by weekend visitors from Barcelona in search of a change of scenery, though the area's popularity with German tourists has also earned it the nickname *Costa dels Alemanys*. Behind the coast the countryside is known as Catalonia's market garden, where fruit and vegetables and the region's famous carnations are grown.

The coastal highway begins just south of Blanes, near the town of Malgrat de Mar. Next comes Pineda de Mar, where the remains of a Roman aqueduct can be seen. The road continues through a succession of old fishing villages, now almost completely given over to tourism. Sant Pol de Mar is an attractive village with a marina, sandy beaches and a 12th-century hilltop monastery, while Canet de Mar is known for its Modernist architecture. Arenys de Mar, an hour out of Barcelona, is still a working fishing port, with a daily fish market by the harbour, a long tradition of white bobbin-lace-making and a shady Rambla leading up to the town. Near here is Caldes d'Estrac, a spa town since Roman times. Finally you reach Mataró, the capital of the region; beyond here are the suburbs of Barcelona. South of Mataró, at Vilassar de Mar, is the flower market where the florists along Barcelona's Ramblas come to buy their wares.

✚ 19M 🚌 From Blanes to most of the resorts 🚂 From Blanes to Calella de la Costa in summer ❓ Markets: Arenys de Mar, Sat; Caldes d'Estrac, Fri; Calella de la Costa, Sat; Canet de Mar, Wed; Malgrat de Mar, Thu; Pineda de Mar, Fri; flower market at Vilassar de Mar, Mon, Wed, Fri 9–1, 3–5

LLORET DE MAR

Fifty years ago Lloret de Mar was still a fishing village; now it has been transformed into a pulsating resort whose population rises to 200,000 in summer and where it is easier to get a hamburger than a Spanish meal. The main thoroughfare, Carrer la Riera, is a non-

stop strip of discos, bars and amusement arcades. Since the 1990s there have been attempts to change Lloret's image, but that seems to be missing the point. If you want fun in the sun, there's no better place.

The main attraction is the beach. The best sheltered swimming is at the north end, beneath the mock castle on the smaller beach of Sa Caleta. Several more beaches are within easy reach – Cala Gran and Cala Canyelles to the north, Platja de Fenals and Santa Cristina to the south. This last is the setting for a traditional festival each July, when the people of Lloret make a pilgrimage by boat, carrying a statue of their patron saint to the hermitage bearing her name. The old town lies just behind the promenade. Look for the 16th-century parish church, with its unusual *Modernista* tiled roof.

✚ 19L 🍴 El Trull (€€€, ➤ 181) 🚌 From Blanes, Girona and Tossa de Mar 🛳 To other south coast resorts in summer ❓ Market on Tue; Festa de Santa Cristina, 24–26 Jul

ℹ Passeig Camprodón y Arrieta 1–2, tel: 972 36 47 35; www.lloretdemar.org

a drive along the coast from Lloret de Mar

This drive takes in the most dramatic stretch of coast road in the Costa Brava.

Start at the car park at the north end of the beach, beside the sardana statue. Take the road that leads uphill, away from the sea, and turn right at the traffic lights towards Tossa de Mar.

Once you leave Lloret the road begins to climb, and there are various *miradors* where you can pull over and admire the sea views. After passing through Tossa de Mar (► 54–55) the road twists and turns through a dizzying series of bends, with cork woods to your left and cliffs dropping into the sea on your right.

> *Follow this coast road for 20km (12.5 miles), then turn right into Sant Feliu de Guíxols (► 168–169). Turn left along the seafront and left again at the end of the beach, following signs to Platja d'Aro. Pass through the centre of this resort (► 166–167) and continue to Sant Antoni de Calonge, where you turn left towards Calonge (► 160–161).*

From Calonge a minor road winds its way through the forest to the pottery town of La Bisbal (► 95).

> *Reaching La Bisbal, turn right towards Palafrugell. Keep on this road as it bypasses Palafrugell and continues south towards Palamós (► 166).*

Keep going south on the coast road from Palamós, retracing your route from Sant Antoni de Calonge. The views along the corniche from Sant Feliu to Tossa are completely different when seen from the other direction.

Distance 130km (80 miles)
Time 4 hours
Start/end point Lloret de Mar ✚ 19L
Lunch Bahía (€€, ► 182), Sant Feliu de Guíxols
☎ 972 32 02 19

PALAMÓS

This fishing port at the eastern end of Palamós bay was founded in 1277 and soon became an important naval base: when the Aragonese fleet conquered Sicily in 1299, it sailed from Palamós. In the 19th century Palamós was the chief export harbour for Catalonia's cork industry, and despite tourism the town retains a significant commercial base today. The fishing fleet still sails daily from Palamós and its arrival each afternoon is followed by a lively fish auction by the harbour.

The old quarter, dominated by the Gothic church of Santa Maria, stands on a headland overlooking the harbour. Several shops here specialize in cork artefacts. A former warehouse on the dockside houses the Museu de la Pesca (Fishing Museum), with exhibits exploring the town's seafaring traditions. The museum offers boat trips around the bay on an old lateen sailing vessel, *Rafael*, built in 1915.

🕇 22J 🍴 La Gamba (€€€, ➤ 182) 🚌 From Girona, Palafrugell and Platja d'Aro 🚢 To other south coast resorts in summer ❓ Market on Tue; carnival, week before Lent; Mare de Déu del Carme, procession of fishing boats 16 Jul 🛈 Passeig del Mar s/n, tel: 972 60 05 50; www.palamos.cat/turisme

PLATJA D'ARO

The small fishing harbour of the village of Castell d'Aro has grown over the last 50 years into the Costa Brava's second largest resort, with a population that rises from 3,000 in winter to more than 100,000 in summer. The beach is 3km (2 miles) of golden sand; the nightlife is legendary and there are numerous activities for children. From discos to watersports, whatever you want in Platja d'Aro is probably there – except peace and quiet.

The original village survives 3km (2 miles) inland, with a medieval castle where art exhibitions are sometimes held, and a Museu de la Nina (Doll Museum). For those who want to escape from the beach, there are free guided walking tours of the old village throughout the year.

🚌 22J 🍴 Fanals Platja (€€–€€€, ➤ 182) 🚍 From Girona, Palamós and Palafrugell ⛴ To other south coast resorts in summer ❓ Market on Fri; carnival, week before Lent

ℹ Carrer Verdaguer 4, tel: 972 81 71 79

S'AGARÓ

This exclusive villa development, on a headland between the beaches of Sant Pol and Sa Conca, was begun around 1924, when industrialist Josep Ensesa commissioned architect Rafael Masó to design the first houses. Built in his classical *noucentista* style, the resort is an attractive mix of Italianate villas, landscaped gardens and a coastal promenade around a succession of rocky coves. Masó's work was completed in the 1940s by Francesc Folguera, who designed the neo-baroque church at the centre of the resort. Film stars and politicians have long flocked to S'Agaró's famous hotel, Hostal de la Gavina, designed by Masó as a Gothic villa and given a more austere classical style by Folguera. Like the rest of the resort, the hotel is elegant and attractive, but has an air of exclusivity that can be off-putting.

🚌 21K 🍴 Beachside restaurants at Platja Sant Pol (€€); Hostal de la Gavina (€€€)

SANT FELIU DE GUÍXOLS

This used to be the Costa Brava's busiest resort. It's a handsome and dignified town, where most of the building took place before the 1960s high-rise boom. Fishing and boat-building are important industries, and during the 19th century the town grew rich on the export trade in cork. The elegant Modernist buildings on the seafront are a reminder of this wealth: look out for Casino la Constancia, a Moorish-style edifice with arches, mosaics and turrets and an old-style cafe on the ground floor.

Sant Feliu grew up around its Benedictine monastery, of which all that remains is the Porta Ferrada, a pre-Romanesque atrium with horseshoe arches. The **Museu d'Història de la Joquina** (toy museum), housed in a small palace, has a collection of more than 3,000 pieces dating back to the 19th century.

The main beach is a wide arc of sand with a fishing harbour at its north end. From the beachfront promenade, Rambla Vidal with its toy museum leads into the old town of narrow streets and squares. The market square contains an unusual 1929 market hall, with art deco touches and bright stained glass. From the southern end of the beach, a road climbs 2km (1.2 miles) to the chapel of Sant Elm. A tourist "train" runs up here regularly in summer.

➕ 21K 🍴 Bahia (€€, ➤ 182) 🚌 From Girona, Palafrugell and Palamós
🚢 To other south coast resorts in summer ❓ Market on Sun; carnival procession, Sun before Lent; Mare de Déu del Carme, procession of fishing boats on 16 Jul
ℹ️ Plaça del Mercat, tel: 972 82 00 51

Museu d'Història de la Joquina

✉️ Rambla Vidal 48–50 ☎ 972 82 22 49 🕐 Mid-Jun to mid-Sep daily 10–1, 5–9; mid-Sep to mid-Jun Tue–Fri 10–1, 4–7, Sat 10–1, 4–8, Sun 11–2
💵 Inexpensive

SERRA DE MONTSENY

The Montseny mountain range is an attractive region of cork, pine and beech forests, villages and mountain streams, straddling the border between Girona and Barcelona provinces, just inland from the southern Costa Brava. It's well known for its springs: much of the country's mineral water is bottled here, especially in the spa town of Sant Hilari Sacalm.

There are two routes into the Serra de Montseny from the coast. Both involve heading for the A7 motorway, which you can leave at the junctions for either Hostalric or Sant Celoni. A circuit of the region, beginning at Hostalric and returning via Sant Celoni, would make a good full-day excursion from one of the south coast resorts.

Hostalric is a medieval walled village, perched on a basalt rock and surrounded by cork forests; a short drive west leads to Breda, known for its pottery shops. The road continues north to Arbúcies, where there is a museum of local crafts in the porticoed town square, before snaking through the mountains to the charming village of Viladrau. From here there is a choice of routes south to Sant Celoni – one via Seva, through the village of Montseny itself, the other passing the region's highest peak, Turó de l'Home (1,706m/5,597ft). At the hermitage of Santa Fé, beneath Turó de l'Home, there is an information centre and a choice of several waymarked walks. Here you are at the heart of the Serra de Montseny nature reserve, and you may see peregrines, eagle owls and red squirrels.

✚ 14L 🍴 Can Barrina (€€), Carretera de Palautordera Sur, Km 1.2, Montseny
🚌 From Girona to Sant Hilari Sacalm ❓ Markets in Arbúcies, Breda and Sant
Hilari Sacalm, Sun; Living Via Crucis, re-enactment of Christ's crucifixion on
Good Friday, Sant Hilari Sacalm; Enramades, ancient festival of floral art on the
Sun after Corpus Christi, Arbúcies; Festa del Flabiol, flute festival in Arbúcies,
late Oct

Parc Natural de Serra de Montseny
ℹ️ Fontmartina, Santa Fé, tel: 938 47 51 02

TOSSA DE MAR
Best places to see, ➤ 54–55.

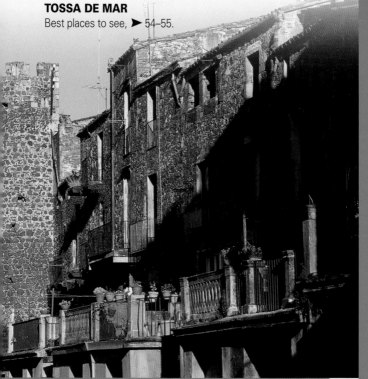

VIC

The opening of the C25 highway, tunnelling through the north of the Montseny mountain range from Girona, brought the ancient market town of Vic within easy reach of the coast. This is a town known even among Catalans as the essence of Catalonia, with an attractive medieval centre containing architecture from Roman to Modernist, enclosed by a ring road on the site of the old city walls.

The best time to visit Vic is on a market day (Tuesday or Saturday), when the main square, Plaça Major, is buzzing with life. Fruit and vegetables are sold at one end, flowers at the other, while the arcades around the edges shelter everything from baby chicks to second-hand books. Stalls at the centre of the square sell bric-a-brac, pottery, household utensils and cheap clothes, and a crafts and wholefood market is set up in the neighbouring square, Plaça del Pes. The butchers and sausage-makers on Carrer dels Argenters do a brisk business (Vic has long been renowned for its *fuet* and *botifarra* sausages) and the streets of the old town echo with gossip. By 3pm the bars are full and the market has been cleared away; by 4pm the cleaners have done their job, the cafes have put out their chairs and you can sit in the sun and appreciate Plaça Major as it is the rest of the week, with pigeons in the square, children playing in the sand and no sign that a market has taken place at all.

✚ 13J

ℹ Ciutad 4, tel: 938 86 20 91

Catedral

Vic's cathedral was begun in the 11th century, but the present building dates from 1803, when the Romanesque belltower was incorporated into a new neoclassical design. Parts of the original cloister survive, with a 14th-century Gothic cloister on top. The most unusual feature is the set of wall paintings by the Catalan mural artist Josep Maria Sert. His first paintings were damaged by fire during the Spanish Civil War and the replacements were inaugurated only days before his death in 1945. The striking red and gold colours and apocalyptic Biblical scenes form a powerful link between the persecution suffered by Christ and that felt by Catalonia at the hands of Spain. Sert is buried in the cloisters. A few of the remaining pieces from his first decoration of the cathedral are displayed in the Capella de la Pietat, a baroque chapel on Carrer Cardona.

⊠ Plaça de la Catedral ☎ 938 86 44 49 ⊕ Daily 10–1, 4–7 ✋ Free (cloister and crypt inexpensive)

Museu de l'Art de la Pell

Tanning is one of Vic's traditional industries, and the Leather Museum, housed in a former convent, contains an unusual collection of thousands of artefacts made totally or partially from leather from around the world. There are chopstick holders from China, funerary face masks from Cameroon, embossed armchairs from Portugal, suitcases from Peru, shadow puppets from Thailand, religious paintings from Spain and a riding saddle from Mexico, all collected by Andreu Colomer i Munmany.

⊠ Carrer Arquebisbe Alemany 5 ☎ 938 83 32 79 ⊕ Tue–Sat 11–2, 5–8, Sun 11–2 ✋ Free

Museu Episcopal

The diocesan museum contains more than 20,000 exhibits, including the most complete collection of Catalan Romanesque art outside Barcelona. The treasures on display include frescoes and altarpieces from remote Pyrenean churches, and some wonderfully lifelike 12th-century wooden statues of the Virgin. Also here are Gothic religious paintings by some of Catalonia's finest artists, including Lluís Borrassa, Bernat Martorell and Jaume Huguet.

✉ Plaça Bisbe Oliba 3 ☎ 938 86 93 60 🕓 Apr–Sep Tue–Sat 10–7, Sun 10–2; Oct–Mar Tue–Fri 10–1, 3–6, Sat 10–7, Sun 10–2 ✋ Moderate

Plaça Major

Vic's main square is one of the most perfect in Catalonia, where buildings of different styles and ages come together, linked by the uneven arches around their base, to create a satisfying whole. This has always been, above all else, a market place; but to experience its symmetry and beauty, come back when it is empty. Within the square are the Gothic town hall, begun in 1388, and buildings from the Renaissance, baroque and Modernist periods.

🍴 Café Nou (€, ➤ 184)

a walk around Vic

The city authorities have created a *ruta turística* around the old town of Vic. By following this simple walk you get to see all the city's main monuments in a short space of time.

Start at the railway station (the bus station is 100m/110yds from here). Walk down Carrer de Jacint Verdaguer, directly opposite the station entrance, leading to Plaça Major.

The tourist office is close to the town hall, directly ahead of you on the far side of the square. If it is open, pick up the leaflet about the town trail, with descriptions of the various buildings along the way. If not, simply follow the signs marked *Ruta Turística*.

Follow the route by heading down Carrer de la Ciutat behind the town hall, then turning right on to Carrer Miquel de Sants.

Continue on this route as it passes historic houses and baroque churches, as well as a Romanesque bridge, a section of the old city walls and a 2nd-century Roman temple. Eventually you return to Plaça Major, where you can stop for a coffee before returning to the station by a different route.

Go down Carrer dels Argenters, the narrow lane in one corner of the square with Forn Sant Miquel on the corner. Reaching a small square, turn left into Carrer de les Escales and go down the steps to reach Rambla del Passeig. Turn left and follow the Ramblas along the course of the old city walls. Turn right when you reach Carrer de Jacint Verdaguer to return to the station.

Distance 3km (2 miles)
Time 1.5 hours
Start/end point Vic station ✚ 13J
🚌 From Girona to nearby bus station
Lunch La Taula (€€, ➤ 184)

HOTELS

BLANES

Horitzó (€€€)

With an excellent location on the beachfront, close to the town centre, this modern, six-storey hotel offers all the comforts; rooms with a balcony overlooking the sea, an international restaurant, swimming pool, sauna, jacuzzi and gym, and a pleasant and relaxed atmosphere.

✉ Passeig Sabadell 11 ☎ 972 33 04 00; www.hotelhoritzo.com

CALONGE

Park Hotel San Jorge (€€€)

Four-star hotel overlooking a rugged stretch of coastline, with access on foot to a pair of secluded coves with crystal clear water. A range of sports is on offer, including tennis, horseback riding and golf.

✉ Carretera de Palamós ☎ 972 65 23 11; www.parkhotelsanjorge.com

LLORET DE MAR

Excelsior (€€)

This seaside hotel features a spa, an excellent restaurant and a terrace on the palm-lined promenade. Most of the 45 rooms have sea views.

✉ Passeig Jacint Verdaguer 16 ☎ 972 36 41 37; www.excelsiorhotellloret.com

Gran Hotel Monterrey (€€)

Luxury hotel on the outskirts of the resort, with a swimming pool and tennis courts in extensive grounds.

✉ Carretera Blanes-Tossa de Mar ☎ 972 34 60 54: www.ghmonterrey.com

Santa Marta (€€€)

Smart, modern hotel set in a pine wood behind the quiet cove of Santa Cristina, with acres of flower gardens and stunning sea views.

✉ Platja Santa Cristina ☎ 972 36 49 04; www.hotelsantamarta.com
🕓 Closed Dec–Jan

PALAMÓS

La Fosca (€)

Modest but comfortable two-star *pension*, set back from the beach in its own quiet bay.

✉ Passeig de la Fosca 24 ☎ 972 60 10 71

Trias (€€)

Luxury and elegance go hand in hand in this modern beach hotel, whose facilities include a swimming pool and solarium.

✉ Passeig del Mar ☎ 972 60 18 00; www.hoteltrias.com

PLATJA D'ARO

Platja Park (€€)

Busy, four-star hotel in the centre of town, with a children's pool and play area and a programme of nightly entertainment. The beach is about 10 minutes' walk away.

✉ Avinguda de Strasburg 10 ☎ 972 81 68 05 🕓 Closed 16 Nov–19 Feb

S'AGARÓ

Hostal de la Gavina (€€€)

The most famous hotel on the Costa Brava was opened in 1924 and designed by the Catalan Modernist architect Rafael Masó in the style of a Gothic villa. Film stars such as Orson Welles and Elizabeth Taylor have stayed here.

✉ Plaça de la Rosaleda ☎ 972 32 11 00; www.lagavina.com 🕓 Closed 2 Jan–3 Apr

S'Agaró (€€)

Less exclusive than its famous neighbour, this luxury four-star hotel also has its own extensive gardens, just a short walk from the beach.

✉ Platja Sant Pol ☎ 972 32 52 00; www.sagarotel.com

S'Agaró Mar (€€)

A lovely family hotel with pool, playground and terrace gardens in the pine woods above Sant Pol beach.

✉ Camí de la Caleta ☎ 972 32 11 40 🕓 Closed 2 Jan–24 Apr

SANT FELIU DE GUÍXOLS
Edén Roc (€€)
Large hotel set in its own grounds beside the cove of Port Salvi. Facilities include a swimming pool and a children's playground.

✉ Port Salvi ☎ 972 32 01 00; www.edenrochotel.com ⊙ Closed Jan

Plaça (€€)
Comfortable three-star hotel with balconies overlooking the market square, a short way back from the beach.

✉ Plaça Mercat 22 ☎ 972 32 51 55; www.hotelplaza.org

TOSSA DE MAR
Diana (€€)
Attractive seafront villa, in Modernist style with arched windows, stained glass and a fireplace by Antoni Gaudí in the lounge.

✉ Plaça d'Espanya 6 ☎ 972 34 18 86; www.diana-hotel.com ⊙ Closed Nov–Mar

Gran Hotel Reymar (€€€)
Arguably the smartest hotel in Tossa, with a heated swimming pool and tennis courts and a pleasant garden with lovely views looking down over the Mar Menuda beach.

✉ Platja Mar Menuda ☎ 972 34 03 12; www.ghreymar.com ⊙ Closed Nov–Apr

Mar Menuda (€€)
Peaceful, traditional hotel on the beach of the same name, just around the bay from Tossa's main beach promenade.

✉ Platja Mar Menuda ☎ 972 34 10 00; www.hotelmarmenuda.com ⊙ Closed Nov–Dec

VIC
Ciutat de Vic (€€)
The best choice in town – a smart, modern business hotel on the edge of the historic centre, with a friendly and helpful reception, comfortable function rooms and a good restaurant.

✉ Passatge Can Mastrot ☎ 938 89 25 51; www.nh-hotels.com

Parador de Vic (€€)

This state-run inn was designed in Catalan farmhouse style, and set in a pine grove overlooking a reservoir at the foot of the Montseny mountains. The restaurant serves hearty Catalan stews and fresh angler fish with garlic mayonnaise. There are wonderful views of the mountains from the outdoor swimming pool.

✉ Paratge Bac de Sau, 14km (8.5 miles) from Vic ☎ 938 12 23 23; www.parador.es

RESTAURANTS

BLANES

Buggy (€€)

On the promenade at the northerrn end of the beach, Buggy specializes in fresh fish and seafood.

✉ Passeig Pau Casals 49 ☎ 972 33 60 64 🕓 After Holy Week–Sep Thu–Tue 12–4, 7–12; Oct, Dec–Holy Week Thu–Tue 12–4. Closed Nov

El Port (€–€€€)

See page 59.

El Ventall (€€€)

One of the top restaurants in the area in a country house between Blanes and Lloret de Mar. The cooking is Mediterranean and modern Catalan.

✉ Carretera de Lloret Km 2 ☎ 972 33 29 81 🕓 Wed–Mon lunch and dinner

LLORET DE MAR

Can Bolet (€€)

Serves good simple dishes in basic surroundings with an emphasis on fish, seafood and paella. Popular with the locals.

✉ Carrer Sant Mateu 6 ☎ 972 37 12 37 🕓 Mid-Jul to Aug daily 12–3:30, 8–11:30; Sep to mid-Jul Tue–Sun 12–3:30, 8–11:30

El Trull (€€€)

Popular fish restaurant overlooking a pretty cove with a terrace with a pool in summer.

✉ Cala Canyelles ☎ 972 36 49 28 🕓 Daily 1–4, 8–11

PALAMÓS
La Gamba (€€€)
The best local seafood, simply prepared, on a terrace overlooking the harbour. Specialities are prawns, *suquet* casserole (white fish and potatoes poached in white wine), oven-baked fish and stuffed sea urchins.
✉ Plaça Sant Pere 1 ☎ 972 31 46 33 🕐 Mon–Wed 1–4, 8–11, Thu–Sun 8–11

Maria de Cadaqués (€€€)
Trendy fish restaurant in the centre of town and close to the port, which displays a collection of paintings by local artists on the walls. The fish comes fresh from the local fleet and is cooked simply and well.
✉ Carrer Tauler i Servià 6 ☎ 972 31 40 09 🕐 Tue–Sun lunch, Tue–Sat dinner

PLATJA D'ARO
El Cau del Pernil (€€)
This traditional cellar-bar specializes in ham, as well as several varieties of sausages and charcoal-grilled meat. It's a meat-eater's heaven.
✉ Avinguda S'Agaró 7 ☎ 972 81 72 09 🕐 Wed–Mon lunch and dinner. Closed Tue and second half of Nov

Fanals Platja (€€–€€€)
Seafood restaurant looking out on to the beach. The specialities, including lobster paella, are expensive, but there are more modestly priced delights on the menu.
✉ Passeig Marítim 92 ☎ 972 81 98 26 🕐 Apr–Oct daily lunch and dinner; lunch only in winter

SANT FELIU DE GUÍXOLS
Bahía (€€)
Popular fish restaurant on the promenade. Start with a *pica-pica*, a selection of a dozen fishy *tapas*.
✉ Passeig del Mar 17 ☎ 972 32 02 19 🕐 Daily 12–4, 8–11

Can Salvi (€€)

The emphasis here is on locally caught fish, including anchovies, salmon and sole in Roquefort sauce.

✉ Passeig del Mar 23 ☎ 972 32 10 13 🕐 Fri–Wed 1–4, 8–11. Closed Sun dinner

El Dorado Mar (€€)

Fresh seafood on a terrace overlooking the sea.

✉ Passeig Marítím President Irla 15 ☎ 972 32 62 86 🕐 Daily lunch and dinner

TOSSA DE MAR

La Cuina de Can Simón (€€€)

Michelin-star restaurant in an old cottage near the town walls offering creative modern Catalan cuisine and a gastronomic menu.

✉ Carrer Portal 24 ☎ 972 34 12 69 🕐 Wed–Sun lunch, Wed–Sat dinner. Daily in summer

Minerva (€€)

One of a row of seafood restaurants facing the beach at the north end of the bay.

✉ Avinguda Sant Ramón de Penyafort ☎ 972 34 09 39 🕐 Daily 12–4. Closed Nov–Feb

Santa Marta (€€)

See page 59.

VIC

Art de Coch (€€)

Stylish, elegantly decorated restaurant with a charming garden for outdoor eating. Serves good local Catalan cuisine.

✉ Carrer Sant Miquel dels Sants 1 ☎ 938 86 29 90 🕐 Mon–Wed 9–4, Thu–Sat 9–4, 8–11

Basset (€€)

Features modern variations on traditional Catalan cuisine.

✉ Carrer Sant Sadurní 4 ☎ 938 89 02 12 🕐 Mon–Sat 1–3:30, 8:30–11

Café Nou (€)

Noisy, bustling locals' pub, packed out on market days. The set menu here is one of the best deals anywhere.

✉ Plaça Major 23 ☎ 938 86 25 02 🕐 Tue–Sun 8am–9pm. Closed Nov

El Jardinet (€€)

Catalan cooking with a hint of French in a delightful restaurant in the back streets of the old town.

✉ Carrer dels Corretgers 8 ☎ 938 86 28 77 🕐 Tue–Sun 1–3:30, 8:30–11. Closed last 2 weeks in Feb, first 2 weeks in Sep

La Taula (€€)

Old mansion with a beautiful timbered ceiling in the medieval centre overlooking a small square. There's a good choice of *tapas*, salads and main meals. Salt cod *(bacallà)* dishes, prepared here in six different ways, and lamb are the specialities. The desserts are home-made.

✉ Plaça Don Miquel de Clariana 4 ☎ 938 86 32 29 🕐 Tue–Sun 1–3:30, 9–11. Closed 15 days in Feb, 15 days in Aug

SHOPPING

FOOD AND DRINK
Cal Ramón
See page 64.

Ca'n Vilada

Carrer dels Argenters has several delicatessens selling the local sausages, such as *llonganissa* and *fuet*, made with pork, bacon and black pepper, for which Vic is famous. This shop at the entrance to the lane is one of the best, with pâtés, salads and numerous varieties of sausage.

✉ Placa Major 34, Vic ☎ 938 86 32 59

MARKETS

Blanes – Mon; Caldes de Malavella – Tue; Calonge – Thu; Lloret de Mar – Tue; Palamós – Tue; Platja d'Aro – Fri; Sant Feliu de Guíxols – Sun; Tossa de Mar – Thu; Vic – Tue, Sat

ENTERTAINMENT

CASINO

Casino Lloret

Modern casino with gaming machines, blackjack, roulette and Spanish card games; dinner-dance and cabaret each Saturday evening.

✉ Carrer dels Esports 1, Lloret de Mar ☎ 972 36 61 16 ⊕ Daily 7pm–4am

NIGHTLIFE

The mega-resorts of Lloret de Mar and Platja d'Aro are the nightlife hot spots of the Costa Brava. During the summer, PR people from the top discos tour the streets handing out free tickets to anyone deemed sufficiently young, sexy and hip. Disco fashions change with the seasons, but long-time favourites include Joy at Platja d'Aro and Tropics at Lloret de Mar. Most discos get busy around midnight and close around 5am.

Gran Palace Flamenco and International Show

This offers a great night out, with a flamenco show and performances by international variety artists, with dining and dancing.

✉ On the road from Lloret de Mar to Blanes ☎ 972 36 57 78
⊕ Daily from 8:45pm

La Masia de Tordera

Traditional dinner with a Spanish-style show in an attractive old farmhouse, including performances of flamenco.

✉ Carretera Girona–Tordera ☎ 937 65 00 49; www.lamasiashow.com
⊕ Daily from 8:45pm

MUSIC FESTIVALS

Calonge

Concerts are held in the medieval castle each August.
☎ 972 66 17 14

Sant Feliu de Guíxols

See page 77.

Index

Acknowledgements

The Automobile Association would like to thank the following photographers and companies for their assistance in the preparation of this book.

Abbreviations for the picture credits are as follows – (t) top; (b) bottom; (c) centre; (l) left; (r) right; (AA) AA World Travel Library

Front cover Tossa de Mar, AA/M Chaplow; **back cover** Tiles of fisherman, AA/M Bonnet; **4l** Restaurant, Platja d'Aro, AA/M Chaplow; **4c** Children playing, AA/M Chaplow; **4r** Teatro Museo Dali, Figueres, AA/S Watkins; **5l** Golf, Peralada, AA/M Bonnet; **5c** River Onar through Girona, AA/P Enticknap; **6/7** Cadaqués, AA/M Bonnet; **8/9** Pottery for sale, Nijar, AA/M Chaplow; **10/11** Beach at Palamos, AA/M Chaplow; **10c** Medieval House, Pals, AA/P Enticknap; **10bl** Cadaques fisherman, AA/M Chaplow; **10br** Casa-Museo Dali, Portlligat, AA/M Chaplow; **11c** Sant Joan de les Abadesses, AA/M Chaplow; **11b** Costa Brava Beach, AA/M Chaplow; **12/13t** Fish with Romesco sauce, AA/M Chaplow; **12/13b** Restaurant, Plaja d'Aro, AA/M Chaplow; **13t** Pan com tomate, Catalan food, AA/M Chaplow; **13c** Catalan salad, AA/M Chaplow; **13b** Olives, market, Ripoli, AA/P Enticknap; **14t** Tapas Bar, Costa Brava, AA/M Chaplow; **14b** Vin de l'Emporda, AA/M Chaplow; **14/15** Café, near Banyoles, AA/M Chaplow; **15** Crema Catalana, AA/M Chaplow; **16** Diving lesson, AA/C Sawyer; **16/17** Fish market, AA/M Jourdan; **17c** Traditional Catalan meal, AA/J A Tims; **17b** Girona, AA/P Enticknap; **18/19t** Castell Gala Dali, Pubol, AA/M Chaplow; **18/19b** Ceramic pottery, AA/M Chaplow; **19t** El Port de la Selva, AA/M Chaplow; **19c** Beach at San Sebastian, AA/M Jourdan; **20/21** Scenic railway, AA/M Bonnet; **24** Festival Havaneras, AA/M Chaplow; **27** RENFE train, AA/M Bonnet; **28/29** Intercity bus, AA/M Jourdan; **32** Policeman, AA/M Bonnet; **34/35** Teatro Museo Dali, Figueres, AA/S Watkins; **36t** Bridge over River Fluvia, Besalú, AA/M Bonnet; **36b** Medieval streets of Besalú, AA/M Bonnet; **37** Bridge over River Fluvia, Besalu, AA/P Enticknap; **38** Cadaques, AA/M Chaplow; **40** Castell Gala Dali, Pubol, AA/M Chaplow; **40/41** Crypt at Castell Gala Dali, AA/M Chaplow; **41** Dali's Cadillac, Castell Gala Dali, AA/M Chaplow; **42** El Rentador, Castello d'Empuries, AA/M Chaplow; **42/43** Castello d'Empuries, AA/M Chaplow; **44** Girona, AA/P Enticknap; **44/45** Houses, Girona, AA/M Chaplow; **45** Banys Arabs, Girona, AA/M Chaplow; **46** Belltower, Monestir de Sant Pere de Rodes, AA/M Bonnet; **46/47** Sant Pere de Rodes, AA/M Chaplow; **47** Sant Pere de Rodes, AA/M Chaplow; **48/49t** Photographing bird, AA/S Watkins; **48/49b** Parc Natural de l'Aiguamolls de l'Emporda, AA/M Chaplow; **50** Citadel, Roses, AA/S Watkins; **50/51** Roses, AA/M Chaplow; **52/53** Teatre-Museu Dali in Figueres, AA/M Chaplow; **54/55** Tossa de Mar, AA/M Chaplow; **56/57** Golf, Peralada, AA/M Bonnet; **58/59** Tapas Bar, AA/M Jourdan; **59** Card players in Tapas Bar, AA/C Sawyer; **60/61** Family sailing, AA/M Chaplow; **62** Casa de Sola Morales, AA/M Chaplow; **63** Placa Major, Banyoles, AA/M Chaplow; **65** Baskets for sale, AA/M Bonnet; **66/67** Beach, Blanes, AA/M Bonnet; **68** Children playing, AA/M Chaplow; **70/71** Cap de Creus, AA/M Chaplow; **73** Golf, Peralada, AA/M Bonnet; **74/75** Medieval town of Besalu, AA/M Chaplow; **76/77** Orchestra (Cobla), AA/M Bonnet; **78/79** City of Girona, AA/P Enticknap; **81** Volca de Montascopa, near Olot, AA/M Chaplow; **83** Banys Arabs, Girona, AA/M Chaplow; **84** Call Jueu, Girona, AA/M Chaplow; **85** Catedral, Girona, AA/M Chaplow; **86/87** Girona, AA/P Enticknap; **88/89** View along river in Girona, AA/M Chaplow; **90/91** Museo d'Art, Girona, AA/M Chaplow; **91** Museo d'Art, AA/M Chaplow; **92** Restaurant, Girona, AA/M Chaplow; **93** Aiguablava, AA/P Enticknap; **95** Pottery, La Bisbal, AA/M Chaplow; **96** Coastal path, Calella de Palafrugell, AA/M Bonnet; **96/97** Calella de Palafrugell, AA/M Chaplow; **96** Coastal path, Calella de Palafrugell, AA/M Bonnet; **98/99** Castellfolit de la Roca, AA/M Chaplow; **100** Medes Island, AA/M Chaplow; **100/101** Glass bottomed boat tour, AA/M Chaplow; **102/103** Olot, AA/M Chaplow; **103** Olot, AA/M Chaplow; **104/105** Rambla Casal dels Volcans, Olot, AA/M Chaplow; **106** Olot, AA/M Chaplow; **107** Garrotxa Natural Park, Olot, AA/M Chaplow; **109** Pals, AA/M Chaplow; **110** Shopping, AA/K Paterson; **111** Sant Joan de las Abadesses, AA/M Chaplow; **112** Tamariu AA/M Chaplow; **113** Torroella de Montgri, AA/M Chaplow; **114/115** Tamariu beach, AA/M Chaplow; **116** Ullastret, AA/M Chaplow; **129** Serra de l'Albera, AA/M Chaplow; **130/131** Cine-Teatre Jardi, Figueres, AA/M Chaplow; **131** Castell de Sant Ferran, Figueres, AA/M Chaplow; **132/133** Narcis Monturoil, Figueres, AA/M Chaplow; **134** Dali Museum, Figueres, AA/P Enticknap; **137** Cap de Creus, AA/M Chaplow; **138** Castello d'Empuries, AA/M Chaplow; **138/139** Castello d'Empuries, AA/M Chaplow; **140/141** La Escala, AA/P Enticknap; **142** Port de la Selva, AA/M Chaplow; **143** Port Lligat, AA/S Watkins; **144/145** Rosas, AA/M Chaplow; **146** Sant Pere Pescador, AA/M Chaplow; **147** Sant Pere Pescador, beach, AA/M Chaplow; **148/149** Serra de l'Albera, AA/M Chaplow; **157** Montseny, AA/M Chaplow; **158** Blanes, AA/M Chaplow; **159** Windsurfers, AA/A Koupranioff; **160/161** Caldes de Malavella, AA/M Chaplow; **162** Lloret de Mar, AA/M Chaplow; **162/163** Sant Roma in Lloret de Mar, AA/M Chaplow; **164/165** Porta Ferrada, AA/M Chaplow; **166/167** Santa Maria church, Palamos, AA/M Chaplow; **167** Platja d'Aro, AA/M Chaplow; **167** Platja d'Aro, AA/M Chaplow; **168** Coastline, Costa Blanca, AA/M Chaplow; **169** Casino la Constancia in Sant Feliu de Guixols, AA/M Chaplow; **170** Montseny National Park, AA/P Enticknap; **170/171** Serra de Montseny, AA/M Chaplow; **172** Market stall, Vic, AA/M Bonnet; **173** Town Hall, Vic, AA/M Chaplow; **174/175** Josep Maria Sert painting in Vic Cathedral, AA/M Bonnet; **175** Placa Major, Vic, AA/M Bonnet; **176/177** Placa Major, Vic, AA/M Chaplow

Every effort has been made to trace the copyright holders, and we apologise in advance for any accidental errors. We would be happy to apply the corrections in the following edition of this publication.

Sight locator index

This index relates to the maps on the covers. We have given map references to the main sights in the book. Grid references in italics indicate sights featured on the town plan. Some sights within towns may not be plotted on the maps.

Dear Reader

Your comments, opinions and recommendations are very important to us. Please help us to improve our travel guides by taking a few minutes to complete this simple questionnaire.

You do not need a stamp (unless posted outside the UK). If you do not want to cut this page from your guide, then photocopy it or write your answers on a plain sheet of paper.

Send to: **The Editor, AA World Travel Guides, FREEPOST SCE 4598, Basingstoke RG21 4GY.**

Your recommendations...

We always encourage readers' recommendations for restaurants, nightlife or shopping – if your recommendation is used in the next edition of the guide, we will send you a **FREE AA Guide** of your choice from this series. Please state below the establishment name, location and your reasons for recommending it.

_____
_____
_____
_____
_____

Please send me **AA Guide** _____

About this guide...

Which title did you buy?

   AA _____

Where did you buy it? _____

When? <u>m m</u> / <u>y y</u>

Why did you choose this guide? _____

_____
_____
_____
_____

Did this guide meet your expectations?

Exceeded ☐   Met all ☐   Met most ☐   Fell below ☐

Were there any aspects of this guide that you particularly liked? _____

_____
_____
_____

continued on next page...

Is there anything we could have done better? _____

_____

_____

_____

About you...

Name (*Mr/Mrs/Ms*) _____

Address _____

_____

_____ Postcode _____

Daytime tel nos _____

Email _____

Please only give us your mobile phone number or email if you wish to hear from us about other products and services from the AA and partners by text or mms, or email.

Which age group are you in?
Under 25 ☐   25–34 ☐   35–44 ☐   45–54 ☐   55–64 ☐   65+ ☐

How many trips do you make a year?
Less than one ☐   One ☐   Two ☐   Three or more ☐

Are you an AA member? Yes ☐   No ☐

About your trip...

When did you book? m m / y y   When did you travel? m m / y y

How long did you stay? _____

Was it for business or leisure? _____

Did you buy any other travel guides for your trip? _____

If yes, which ones? _____

_____

_____

Thank you for taking the time to complete this questionnaire. Please send it to us as soon as possible, and remember, you do not need a stamp (*unless posted outside the UK*).

> **AA** Travel Insurance call 0800 072 4168 or visit www.theAA.com